The Making of The Railway Children

Researched and compiled for the Keighley & W...

Back in the mists of time when I was Oakworth's ...
around in a Citroen 2CV, I remember a young girl gett...
Unaccustomed to people worshipping the ground I ...
only to discover that I had encountered possibly the w...

Many similar encounters followed and I concluded that the Railway would be well advised to produce a book which described the making of the film, as recalled by the volunteers who were actually there. With the film's 20th anniversary rapidly approaching in 1990, I rashly suggested the idea only to be told that I was a fool and it would never sell.

Fast forward twenty years and we found the railway seeking ways to celebrate the film's 40th anniversary. Older but little wiser I reminded them of my idea for a book and, to my astonishment, was told, 'Just go away and do it'

The first efforts were simple photo-copied affairs which cobbled together a few articles from the Railway's in-house magazine Push & Pull. These were sold on board the Old Gentleman's Saloon where your scribe and partner Christine served Cream Teas on Vintage Train days. They are probably collector's items now - the books, not me and Christine !

Encouraged by this wave of apathy, I produced a 'proper' book which included both existing and much new material. This was published to much critical acclaim in March 2010 and sold out within two years. It had taken twenty years but I finally felt vindicated.

And now more than two years on, much additional information has come to light and fresh contacts made. It therefore seems appropriate to produce an updated edition which hopefully gives a fuller picture of the film's production and lays to rest a few of the myths perpetrated on that work of the devil known as the internet and on the various social networking sites much loved by today's twittering classes.

It has been a privilege to produce this book and I would like to thank the many working members of the railway who have contributed. Advancing years can play tricks with one's memory so some of the recollections may be a bit vague in places, however they remain an invaluable addition to this Railway's history and its proud contribution to what remains a very fine British film.

ﾭﾭﾭﾭﾭﾭﾭﾭ **This book is dedicated to 'Tabitha'** ﾭﾭﾭﾭﾭﾭﾭﾭﾭ

Published by the Keighley & Worth Valley Light Railway Limited, The Railway Station, Haworth, Keighley, West Yorkshire, BD22 8NJ

Copyright – Keighley & Worth Valley Light Railway Limited 2012

First published March 2010

This revised and expanded Second Edition published November 2012

ISBN: 978-0-902438-34-7

Introduction _____ by Ann Cryer

KWVR President ANN CRYER recalls how it all began and how she and her family became 'Railway Children'

My late husband, Bob Cryer, was a man of many interests. In addition to his passion for the preservation of the Worth Valley Railway, he also played in Bradford League cricket, made 9.5mm cine films, was involved in politics, and was a member of the Armstrong Siddeley Owners Club. He wasn't cut out for taking a semi-detached interest in anything; it was hands-on stuff and we, his family, fitted in around his various preoccupations.

ABOVE – Ann mingles with the stars at Oakworth station – Photo: Bob Cryer

Thus from around 1969 with Bob as Chairman of the KWVR Preservation Society and Film & TV Liaison Officer, and in the absence of a railway telephone, I became its ears and voice via our two-tone green Trimphone dealing with enquiries or, as Perks might say, conversationalising with the general public. I particularly remember a call I took in Autumn 1969: a smooth, polished, slightly theatrical voice introduced himself as Bob Lynn and he was interested in making a feature film of 'The Railway Children". His friend, actor Lionel Jeffries, had seen the BBC television series and his daughter had persuaded him to buy the film rights from the Nesbit estate. Weeks and many phone calls later, this impressive twosome arrived in the Worth Valley and, as Bob explains in his piece written those many years ago, the three of them walked the line with possible locations being indicated and discussed.

They came back to our front room for tea and Lionel did a repeat performance of a discussion he'd had with a family of lineside pigs – another very entertaining story !

In the subsequent months, Bob and I spent much of our free time looking at further possible locations including Three Chimneys, Perks' cottage and Dr. Forrest's House. We also identified two locations on the Leeds & Liverpool Canal for the sequence where the children save a baby from a barge – the Fisherman's Inn at Bingley and a superbly restored narrow boat at Barnoldswick. Sadly this scene was cut from the film to remain within budget but I still have the original script and it clearly shows where Producer Bob Lynn had to block out pages 204 to 242, between the Perks' birthday scenes.

With Bob busy as 'Railway Technical Advisor', I spent a couple of days on the set with our children, John and Jane, as 'extras'. It was the day they were filming the closing shot and we all had to be down there quite early since Lionel wasn't really sure if it would work. They put the big Mitchell camera on one of the Railway's old Wickham Trolleys and pushed it slowly towards the main actors in front of the engine and it worked beautifully. They stored all of the equipment out of shot on the far side of Ebor Lane bridge.

ABOVE – Arthur Ibbetson turns the camera towards Ann and family – Photo: Bob Cryer

Afterwards while Bob was talking to Arthur Ibbetson (Director of Photography) about how it had all gone, he asked, "Would you mind just pretending to shoot Ann and the children with the Mitchell camera so that we can have a photo to remind us of today?" Arthur had grandchildren of his own of about the same age so he had no hesitation in posing and pretending to do the shot.

I remember Bob suggesting to Lionel, "You're not getting enough shots of the engines" and Lionel saying to him, "My dear boy, I know you love your wonderful engines but this film is about more than just engines, and don't worry we have enough shots". Later when Teddy Darvas was doing the editing, he realised that Bob had been right all along and they did have to come back to do some more railway shots.

On 21st December 1970 we went to the newly opened ABC cinema in Shaftesbury Avenue where 'The Railway Children' was being premiered in 'ABC 2' along with 'There's A Girl In My Soup' starring Goldie Hawn and Peter Sellers on 'ABC 1'. The film was also premiered at the Ritz in Keighley where it was so popular that the Railway ran extra trains for cinema-goers.

Following the film's release, the Railway enjoyed a huge boost in traffic. Four years later, Bob became the M.P. for Keighley and in 1976 he was appointed a Junior Minister in Jim Callaghan's government. Inevitably this restricted his Railway activities and he was forced to step down as a steam driver, something he very much regretted. On the plus side it meant that I no longer had to clean the black tide mark from the bath when he'd been on duty.

Advertisements courtesy of the Keighley News

Finally, may I add a personal thank-you to the late Lionel Jeffries whose unsung kindness was to benefit our railway since he decided to retain Oakworth as the name of the station. During a break in filming I told Lionel that we had just seen him in "Chitty Chitty Bang Bang" at the Keighley Ritz cinema. He asked John and Jane what they thought of it, then bent over and sang the title song to them. It made a huge impression which stays with them to this day. He also gave them a close shot in "The saviours of the iron road" presentation scene on Oakworth platform. Two small children waving flags captured forever by Arthur Ibbetson when they were just four and six. This and Bob's screen credit, "Robert Cryer - Technical Adviser", was I'm sure Lionel's thank-you to him for the months of planning and preparation that he had willingly given. Of the many positions Bob held, none pleased him more.

Therefore, Lionel Jeffries, Actor, Director, Scriptwriter and very kind man - thank-you.

LEFT – Bob Cryer and steam locomotive, July 1965
Photo: Robin Higgins

"We were not Railway Children to begin with"

BOB CRYER recalls ....

The late Bob Cryer worked as Railway Consultant to the film makers and wrote this article shortly after the film's release. Bob was one of the Railway's founder members and spent some time as the Member of Parliament for Keighley

Photo: Telegraph & Argus, Bradford

<u>To Begin at the Beginning</u> - The feature film of Edith Nesbit's charming story did not simply spring into being in 1970; its origins may be found in the BBC television serial filmed in 1968, also on the Worth Valley line. In February of that year, the director for the seven part serial, Julia Smith (subsequently the producer for 'EastEnders') was given a diesel railbus ride on the line and agreed that the location was eminently suitable. On Monday 25th March 1968, the complete BBC unit arrived and spent ten hectic days filming. Society members were kept equally busy setting up a fake signal near Oxenhope and sprucing up Oakworth station. This was shortly before the Railway was re-opened and Oakworth station required eight broken windows to be replaced, whilst gas lamps needed new mantles and lanterns. In addition, the station was painted and the fence repaired. Weeds adorned much of the area and these had to be cleared. Quite apart from all this, the three engines, Sir Berkeley, Joem, and No. 31 were prepared for three days of steam engine activity. On Sunday 12th May 1968, the first of the episodes was screened at 5.25pm. An excited crowd of Society members gathered around a television set in Haworth shed. This was, after all, the first real use of our Railway for a nationwide television programme and we were sure that the black and white film would provide a creditable record of our efforts. We all thought the programme quite splendid.

<u>Enter Mr Jeffries</u> - What we did not know was that watching the serial was Lionel Jeffries, the character actor of dozens of British feature films and the occasional big budget spectacular such as 'Chitty Chitty Bang Bang'. His daughter persuaded him to purchase the cinema screen rights and, because he was keen to make his directorial debut, Lionel Jeffries enthusiastically wrote the script and submitted it to Elstree Studios. As the British film industry lurched through another crisis, a new chief executive arrived at the studios in the form of Bryan Forbes, who had already worked with Lionel Jeffries. He like the script, rejected the idea of turning it into a musical, and allocated money for production as part of a ten film programme.

<u>Inspection and Approval</u> - Armed with studio approval, the new director obtained details of our Railway from the BBC and arranged to walk the line, together with producer Bob Lynn and your author. On a fine autumn day in 1969, the line was scrupulously examined and the principal locations were chosen. It was on this convivial occasion that Lionel Jeffries was persuaded to let Oakworth station retain its identity rather than use the name Meadow Vale, as in the BBC series. When the film was exhibited, this helped enormously in pinpointing the

location, which in turn gave such a boost to our passenger figures. Subsequently, many more people made the journey to the Worth Valley to draw up plans for the filming. These included art director John Clarke and cameraman Arthur Ibbetson – the latter's credits included 'Where Eagles Dare' and 'Anne of a Thousand Days'. He had started his distinguished career as a clapper boy on David Lean's 1945 film 'Brief Encounter', centred, as readers may recall, on a railway station and, in fact, filmed at Carnforth. Sound was recorded by long standing railway enthusiast Peter Handford.

Filming Commences - Organisation for the feature film was more sophisticated than for the BBC production. Filming took longer, used more trains more frequently, and involved a much larger budget, though at £350,000 it was relatively economical by 1970 standards. When all the demands of the script had been defined, they were entered into a programme of filming called a 'crossplot'. This diagrammatic record commenced on Monday 6th April with filming of exteriors of a London villa, and concluded on Friday 12th June with interior shots in a railway tunnel. Listed for each day were the location, artists required, 'cabs, carriages, gigs & carts', trains, and the scene numbers to be filmed. In all, there were 15 studio days at Elstree and 39 location days, most of which were on the Worth Valley Railway, though Haworth village, the Parsonage and Wycoller hamlet were also used.

The Trains - Various types of train were discussed and three basic types evolved for different roles in the film.

ABOVE - The ex-GWR pannier tank No. L89 was to be the warm, friendly engine with the smart coaches painted in cream and dark maroon coupled to the wood-grained director's saloon in which the Old Gentleman rode so serenely - Photo: Robin Lush

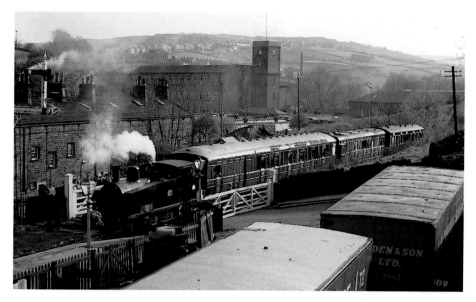

ABOVE - The local train comprised a rather heterogeneous collection of four and six wheeled coaches and was hauled by Manchester Ship Canal locomotive No. 67 – Photo: Robin Lush

BELOW - The Barton Wright tender engine No. 957 was painted green and meant to be a rather fierce express engine, feared by all. So fierce in fact that its thunder and noise cause the landslide which is the centre-piece of the film, and it creates an opportunity for the children to save the following train from disaster – Photo: Robin Lush

Why the KWVR? – At the time, our Railway was the only preserved stretch of line which could provide such a wide range of rolling stock and working locomotives. All those chosen were of Victorian design and, whilst the express seemed a little on the slow side – indeed a mild joke was incorporated into the script to account for this – a branch line with a 25mph speed limit simply could not provide express train speeds. All the liveries used had their basis in contemporary illustrations and were adapted to the needs of the story. Liveries for coaches and locomotives were relatively straightforward. The major problem was getting the relevant trains marshalled each night, prior to filming the following day. If a train was filmed moving left to right at Oakworth station and was subsequently filmed at Haworth, the whole train had to be reversed, because the platform is on the other side of the line. This meant turning the engine at Shipley triangle and changing the coaches to match. Mercifully this was a rare occurrence, but British Rail provided facilities when needed with great efficiency. Whatever the situation, marshalling for the next day's filming rarely concluded before midnight and, if a big engine like the 'N2' was needed, lighting up commenced around 4am so as to be ready for an 8am start. The unit call was normally for 8.30am at the location and daily call sheets were issued detailing all the requirements from teaspoons to trains. When steam engines and trains were not required, but filming was taking place along the line, a diesel railbus took people and equipment to the spot. Alternatively this would be left to D226 plus a wagon and electrical generating equipment to power the arc lights invariably used, even though the weather throughout was superb.

ABOVE - The 'Scotch Express' comprising LNER 'N2' 0-6-2 No. 4744 and four bogie coaches whirls through Oakworth station – Photo: Brian Baker

A major location away from the stations was the landslide constructed on the bank in the cutting below Mytholmes tunnel. In the BBC version, a small tree was carried on the locomotive buffer beam to the bend near Oxenhope and supplemented with branches. The cinema version had something rather more spectacular. Three long steel channels were placed in the hillside with three short vertical tubes located in each. These were drawn up the hillside by cables and released to slide down as required. In the two outside tubes were placed small trees and, in the centre one, a rather special fibreglass tree made by the art department at Elstree. On the day of filming, when the centre tree reached its lowest point, the hinged base caused the trunk to fall over whilst, simultaneously, the 40 tons of Fuller's earth and gravel piled up behind sleepers at the bottom of the cutting were exploded, causing this mixture to slide across the track. It was all very expensive and, to this viewer, not particularly effective on the screen. Moreover, there was no opportunity for retakes once the charges were detonated. Perhaps a large tree across the track might have been more realistic and the money saved could have been spent on the canal sequence, where the three children rescue a baby from a burning barge. A location on the Leeds-Liverpool canal near the Fisherman's Inn at Wagon Lane, Bingley, was picked out but, sadly, abandoned because of lack of money.

The Film and its Makers – 'The Railway Children' was, even in 1970, a relatively rare phenomenon; a British financed production using United Kingdom locations which, together with vivacious performances from the leading players, Bernard Cribbins, Dinah Sheridan and William Mervyn and the three children, Jenny Agutter, Sally Thomsett and Gary Warren, created a warm hearted evocation of the more pleasant aspects of late Victorian England. It was the most successful of the ten films made during Bryan Forbes's reign at Elstree. Certainly, a competent directorial debut by Lionel Jeffries, it perhaps lacked the necessary emphasis on the trains which are, after all, the centre-piece of the film. This is not merely my prejudice. When compiling the film, editor Teddy Darvas had to arrange for a further day's filming to provide more engine shots for the averted crash sequence. More film was also needed of the 'Scotch Express' but alas by July the 'N2' had burst a boiler tube and was not available.

"The Green Dragon" near Haworth.   photo: G. W. Morrison

You can ride on the railway used by

"The Railway Children"

E.M.I.'s fine production of "The Railway Children" was filmed on the Worth Valley Railway which runs for five miles between Keighley in Yorkshire through Oakworth and Haworth (home of the Brontes) to Oxenhope.

You can see the engines and coaches actually used in the film and ride on the railway used by the children!

BELOW. Oakworth Station during filming—it is still kept as it was decorated for the film.

Released in December 1970, with a premier in London on 21st December and in Keighley soon after at the then Ritz cinema, where it played to packed houses, the film provided a real stimulus for our Railway. Nothing was left to chance and leaflets spelling out the location and services of the line were distributed wherever The Railway Children played and Society members could gain access. Our Railway has been associated with this, by now, perennial cinema and television favourite ever since, and recently a touring stage play has been doing the rounds, performed by the Birmingham Repertory Company and playing in the provinces to packed houses. Valuable publicity and input was made available by the Railway to this also. People still ask where the railway children lived (at Bent's Farm, Oxenhope), though they watched the trains near Oakworth by cinematic sleight of hand. Renewed interest in this admirable production will, once again, provide a stimulus to passengers and membership.

LEFT – KWVR publicity handout from 1970
Photo: KWVR Archives

The Railway Children at the BBC _____

To date, BBC television has broadcast four serialisations of 'The Railway Children'

In 1951 Dorothea Brooking produced an eight part adaptation which went out at 5.30pm on Tuesday evenings from 6th February to 27th March. Among the cast were John Le Mesurier as Doctor Forrest and Jean Anderson as Mother. These 30 minute live programmes were not recorded but their popularity led to a remake later that year as 4 hour-long episodes using largely the same cast and a mix of new and original material.

Photo: BBC World

In 1957 a completely new version was produced by Dorothea Brooking which remained faithful to the earlier adaptation but included more location filming and railway scenes shot around Baynards station in Surrey on the old Guildford to Horsham line. It was broadcast nationwide and gained the rare honour of featuring on the cover of Radio Times.

Photos: BBC World

In 1968 a new seven part serialisation of the story was broadcast. It was directed by Julia Smith (of EastEnders fame) and featured Jenny Agutter in the role of Bobbie and Gordon Gostelow as Mr Perks. All of the railway scenes were filmed on the K&WVR a few months before the line re-opened. It is certainly a charming and faithful interpretation of the story and is the only version of the series currently available on DVD.

ABOVE – Oakworth became 'Meadow Vale' for the BBC's 1968 series – Photo: Stephen Prior

ABOVE – A youthful Jenny Agutter is seen here clinging to the station clock with other members of the cast and crew. Below her is the series Director Julia Smith who went on to fame as the co-creator and Producer of EastEnders – Photo: Ken Roberts

BELOW – Class J72 No. 69023 on filming duties at Oakworth – Photo: Eric Ring

ABOVE – Jenny Agutter with Gillian Bailey and Neil McDermott – Photo: Hubert Foster

BELOW – Gordon Gostelow (Mr Perks) chats to the children – Photo: Yorkshire Post

KWVR volunteer, Mike Goodall, recalls that 'The Railway Children' filming provided a wealth of incidents, many of which are unrepeatable. The Manchester Ship Canal locomotive No. 31 was in the BBC serial and an attempt to keep smoke and steam to a minimum led to what must be one of the slowest non-stop runs ever recorded between Oakworth and Haworth.

The scene demanded that the train ran downhill into Oakworth station, stopped and then continued after passengers had been discharged. In those days No. 31 did not have vacuum equipment to operate the train brakes, so only the locomotive's steam brake was available to bring things to a halt. Bringing the 95 ton train to a standstill on a steeply falling gradient from a realistic passenger speed, and to within six inches of a marker post, took some doing. The crew were fully intent on this matter as they entered the station. Having succeeded, the driver looked for the guard's signal to set off again. The passengers had disembarked but there was no sign of the guard. After an embarrassing delay, the producer called 'cut'. Unhappily, nobody had told the guard about his role in the scene. Hurriedly, because of failing light, it was decided to re-take the scene and this time the guard was on cue. The train re-started and set off down the line towards Damems. Stopping on the curves between the two stations the driver noticed that the boiler pressure had fallen somewhat. A glance in the firebox revealed the cause. In order to cut down the noise, No. 31 had been run on a very thin fire which needed regular attention – attention it had not received during the mix-up over the last shots.

Back at Oakworth the film crew had packed up. "We'll propel the train back to Haworth so take it easy" was an instruction that was hardly necessary, With only 60 pounds on the pressure gauge, No. 31 set off up the bank at a very sedate pace indeed. Over Mytholmes viaduct the driver espied a member walking in the same direction. "Hop on" he offered, but the member preferred to walk. Through Mytholmes tunnel, round the curve to Ebor Lane, and up the long straight towards Haworth, No. 31 thundered along at all of three miles an hour. Finally as she passed Haworth platform ramp, the pedestrian came into view having kept pace with the train by walking behind it. Bidding a polite farewell, he overtook the train and vanished through the booking hall before it eventually wheezed to a halt, finishing a poor second.

LEFT – Class J72 No. 69023 and train approach Oxenhope during filming. Note the dummy signal erected during the filming.

Photo: KWVR Archive

The Film Cast

Producer: Robert Lynn   Director: Lionel Jeffries   Screenplay: Lionel Jeffries
Music: Johnny Douglas   Director of Photography: Arthur Ibbetson B.S.C.

Photo: Howard Malham

Mother	Dinah Sheridan
Mr Perks	Bernard Cribbins
The Old Gentleman	William Mervyn
Father	Iain Cuthbertson
Bobbie	Jenny Agutter
Peter	Gary Warren
Phyliss	Sally Thomsett
Doctor	Peter Bromilow
Ruth	Ann Lancaster
Shabby Russian	Gordon Whiting
Aunt Emma	Beatrix Mackey
Mrs Perks	Deddie Davies
Bandmaster	David Lodge
Jim	Christopher Witty
Mrs. Viney	Brenda Cowling
Cart Man	Paddy Ward
Photographer	Eric Chitty
Maid	Sally James
C.I.D. Man	Dominic Allen

Edith Nesbit

'The Railway Children' author, Edith Nesbit, was born in 1858 at 38 Lower Kennington Lane in London. The daughter of John Collis Nesbit, she was the youngest of five children and known to her family as 'Daisy'.

She spent her early years moving between France and England, unhappily attending a succession of boarding schools. In 1871 the family moved back to England and rented Halstead Hall in Kent where Edith and her brothers used to play near the railway line – a memory which was to inspire her future writing.

At the age of 21 and while seven months pregnant, Edith married bank clerk Hubert Bland. They shared a love of poetry and collaborated on many projects throughout a turbulent relationship where both partners openly conducted extra-marital affairs. Apart from her own two children, she brought up several that Bland fathered with his mistresses.

They were both socialists and involved in the Fabian Society from its inception - even naming one of their children Fabian after their joint interest. Nesbit befriended several of its members, including George Bernard Shaw (with whom she had an affair) and H.G. Wells. Adopting a nonconformist style, she cut her hair short, smoked heavily and wore less restrictive clothing than Victorian fashion dictated. Inspired by the Fabians' ideals, she wrote and lectured on socialism throughout the 1880s.

When Bland's business ventures failed, Nesbit became the main breadwinner and undertook other work to finance their growing household. She became a successful children's writer with novels including The Story of the Treasure-Seekers (1899), The Wouldbegoods (1901), Five Children and It (1902), The Phoenix and the Carpet (1904), The Railway Children (1906), and The Enchanted Castle (1907). Her works were credited to 'E. Nesbit' and early reviewers often assumed the writer to be a man. Hubert Bland also collaborated with Nesbit on her writing, much of it being serialised in the 'London Weekly Dispatch' under the alias 'Fabian Bland'.

After the death of Hubert Bland in 1914, Edith married ship's engineer Thomas Tucker. She continued to write children's books but years of heavy smoking took their toll and she succumbed to lung cancer in 1924 at the age of 65, having published a total of 44 novels. She was buried in the little churchyard of St Mary's in the Marsh in Dymchurch.

'The Railway Children' is probably the best known of Nesbit's many children's stories and was originally serialised in 'The London Magazine' during 1905 and published in book form in 1906, since which it has never been out of print. The best known version of the story is undoubtedly Lionel Jeffries' 1970 film and it is of note that the original episodic nature of the story remains evident in the film.

The Edith Nesbit Society ('www.edithnesbit.co.uk') aims to celebrate the life and work of the author and her friends with talks, publications, and a regular newsletter.

"The pretty life at Edgecombe Villa" _____

Some of the opening scenes were shot at Elstree's Borehamwood studio, while others used an empty house in Hampstead which was dressed with period fittings under the expert eye of Art Director John Clark. Here we meet the Waterbury family, Ruth the maid, Great Aunt Emma and Potts the dog. The children live a happy life until one fateful day when two grim-faced gentlemen call to see Father. To their great horror he is arrested and taken away and life becomes very different indeed. Mother subsequently tells the children that Father has been unexpectedly called away on business and arranges for the strict Aunt Emma to help out for a while before she goes abroad to work as a Governess. The days that follow are very strange, with Mother away for long periods. Then one day she returns with important news; they must be very brave and 'play at being poor for a while'. She has made arrangements for them to move to a 'darling little house' in the country. Old and picturesque, it stands next to a sleepy old railway line ....

ABOVE - Playing trains' between takes at Edgecombe Villa - Photo: Canal + Image UK Ltd

BELOW – The children play in the kitchen with Ruth the maid - Photo: Canal + Image UK Ltd

Mr. and Mrs. Waterbury at 'Edgecombe Villa' in Hampstead, the empty house which was used in many of the early scenes – Photo: Canal + Image UK Ltd

"To a darling little house in the country" ____

Following Father's arrest, the family move to the country and live in a house near the railway called 'Three Chimneys'

ABOVE – The family arrive at Oakworth station – Photo: Canal + Image UK Ltd.

Having struggled off the train with their heavy bags, the family meet a rather stern man driving a horse and cart who shows them the way up to 'Three Chimneys'. The part was played by Paddy Ward, who also starred in the BBC's 1957 TV serialisation.

Photo: Canal + Image UK Ltd.

"Send our love to Father" _____

The children often ran down from Three Chimneys to wave to the train, asking it to "send our love to Father". This was a little bit of filming magic as the two locations are about two miles apart. Three Chimneys is above Oxenhope station, while the fence where the children waved is near Mytholmes tunnel between Haworth and Oakworth – Photos: Canal + Image UK Ltd.

"Right away, Mr. Mitchell" _____

KWVR volunteer and former Society Chairman, GRAHAM MITCHELL, describes how he landed a speaking role in the film.

Back in 1970, I was in my fifth year as a junior master at Dudley Grammar School and was commuting to the Railway a couple of times a month to work as a volunteer. I'd been a Working Member since 1968 and having just qualified as a guard, I was very keen to do every turn that was available to me. It was therefore fortunate that the May half term holidays coincided with a call for volunteers to help with some filming work on the railway. I was available for the whole week, so it was my great luck to be chosen for the part of Guard in the film. Almost all of the sequences involving the train departures and arrivals from Oakworth were being shot during that particular week and there I was; as a newly passed out guard I got the opportunity.

ABOVE – Guard Graham Mitchell awaits the 'Right Away' at Oakworth while talking to 'The Old Gentleman' William Mervyn – Photo: Canal + Image UK Ltd.

For my efforts I was paid the princely sum of seven pounds and fifteen shillings - a tidy sum given that my monthly net wage at that time as a qualified graduate teacher was only sixty pounds a month. I don't know if I was paid extra because I had a small speaking part, I was just glad to get the money and said "Thank you very much."

The excellent script is worthy of note, though certainly anyone familiar with Nesbit's book will understand that it bears little relationship to the words actually spoken in our classic film. This may be due in part to the close working relationship between Lionel Jeffries and Bernard

Cribbins who had acted together in many classic comedy films and clearly trusted each other as fellow professionals. This was Lionel's first film as a director and I think he simply trusted Bernard to get on with it. Most of the wonderful lines we remember like, "I've never seen anything more like a buttercup 'cepting it were a buttercup", "What's that squirrel doin' ont' table", and "It's all uphill to Scotland" are, I believe, all pure Cribbins ad-libs. I certainly never saw anything remotely resembling a script, though presumably the main actors all had them. Consequently, when we got to the train departure sequence, I was asked what we would normally do to take the train out. I explained that it was the duty of the station foreman to give the tip and discussed with Bernard what he would say as Mr Perks. He therefore says "Right away Mr Mitchell" and the guard responds "Thank you Mr Perks". It was actually made up on the spur of the moment, as were many of Bernard's lines, but it worked perfectly and we did it correctly because I explained how it should be done on a railway and we stuck to it.

My grand flourish of the green flag came about because they said, "Be slightly larger than life". Now as a shy and retiring 27 year old who had yet to develop the exuberant personality of later years, this did not come easily so I simply put a little extra flourish into that particular take and it seemed to work. The director liked it and that scene was in the can.

LEFT – William Mervyn 'The Old Gentleman' relaxes in between takes - Photo: Robin Higgins

Over the years, many journalists have asked, "What was it like working with Jenny Agutter?" They of course forget that Jenny and the other young actors Sally Thomsett and Gary Warren were relatively unknown then. The real stars at the time were comedy actor Bernard Cribbins and the fabulous Dinah Sheridan who had enjoyed a huge success a few years previously in the film 'Genevieve'. I also enjoyed sharing my train with the wonderful William Mervyn as The Old Gentleman, who was already well known through the hugely popular TV programme 'All Gas and Gaiters'. Cameras and microphones are a common enough sight in the Worth Valley these days but forty years ago it was a huge novelty to have a big film unit here and to see those big name stars here in our little villages and on our railway. People turned up just to see them, watch them filming and get their autographs, and the children were not really the focus of very much attention.

Continuity can throw up all sorts of problems. On the Sunday evening following my week on the railway, I got a phone call from the Assistant Director saying "We must have you back on set tomorrow as we've got to re-shoot some of your scenes". Now film companies live on a different planet to the rest of us and seemed unconcerned that I had to be back teaching at 9am on the Monday morning. Not wishing to incur the wrath of my very traditional headmaster, I suggested that the Assistant Director should make the approach. I was duly telephoned by my Headmaster who said, "Ah Mitchell, I have been approached by a theatrical personage who has asked me to allow you to take time off to appear in some sort of film, I suppose you'd better go then." I nervously thanked him and summoned a taxi to Wolverhampton station where I caught a train to Manchester Piccadilly, to be met by a chauffeur driven car and conveyed back to my parent's home. I appeared on set on Monday and all the scenes were re-shot. Sadly these all ended up on the cutting room floor, but that's life in the world of films. Incidentally, my headmaster didn't actually speak to me for about a month after this incident.

Anyone who has been involved in filming work will know that it can involve an awful lot of sitting around doing very little for an awfully long time. I recall sitting in the Old Gentleman's Saloon with William Mervyn awaiting instructions from the production crew. After about three hours, William was getting restless and walked down the line to accost Lionel Jeffries. "Look, do you actually want us or not this morning - 'cos if you don't want us I'm taking this bloody train and were going to have some lunch". With permission duly granted, the entire train repaired to Haworth whereupon William Mervyn, still in costume, made a beeline for the Royal Oak. "A flagon of ale for my companions, landlord, if you please". The train crew of course did not enjoy his hospitality for they were very definitely on duty, but I do remember William Mervyn and his friends enjoying a very merry afternoon.

ABOVE - Left to right: Jenny Agutter, Sally Thomsett, William Mervyn, Gary Warren, Bob Phizackerley (Driver), Graham Mitchell (Guard), Paul Waite (Fireman) - Photo: Ian Walker

The film's impact should not be underestimated. It enlivened the whole valley, and staff at Keighley's Ritz cinema had to seek out their 'House Full' notices when it was premiered there. There was a fantastic joy in and love of this film. It was our film, made in our valley, with our people, and on our railway. An elderly gentleman in Oakworth once said to me, "You know what's so great about that there film? It's got no drugs, no drinking, no sex, no bad language and no folk running round wi' no clothes on." And he was right for it's really a moral tale of good triumphing over evil, and it shows how a film can be a great film without having 'sex, drugs and rock and roll'. The film critic, Barry Norman, rated it the greatest British children's film ever made, and that's a fantastic compliment and a great triumph for this valley and for the railway.

My involvement with the filming was largely concentrated into that one week and it was clearly difficult to imagine how it would look on screen because you are just doing a series of short unconnected sequences in what is perhaps a two hour film. You don't understand the bigger picture until you finally see it on the screen. At the time it was a jolly romp with wonderfully interesting and famous people which caused great excitement in the area. I don't think any of us could have dreamt how it would turn out or the huge success it would become.

The impact upon the railway over the past forty years has been tremendous. I can think of no other single happening on the railway which has had such a big and lasting impact as the making of that film. I don't think that there was ever a day during the thirty-odd years that I was a working member on this railway when somebody didn't come up to me and mention the film. Some people have commented that I'm always talking about the film; that is simply not true. I never raise the subject, it is always other people who bring it up. I recall one man came up to me on Haworth Station after I retired and said, "I know you, you're that chap who used to be Graham Mitchell and you were in that Railway Children film".

ABOVE – William Mervyn with KWVR volunteer driver Nick Hellewell at Oxenhope station while the pannier tank takes water – Photo: Ian Walker

What people forget is that over the last 40 years, most of my age group on the railway have actually been involved in literally scores of short film scenes, mainly for TV. I and others have also "trod the boards" in lots of school and local 'Am Dram' productions, and still turn out for the occasional choice cameo role. So the fact that the 1970 film role continues to dog me after forty years remains something of a mixed blessing; I think it's called 'type-casting' so "Thank you, Mr. Perks".

"Why's it going so slowly Mr. Perks?" _____

After seven months at sea as an engineer, KWVR volunteer DERRICK BEGG returned to Haworth to find a notice requesting loco crews for the filming trains. He put his name down and has many memories of that long hot summer.

The Scotch Flyer

I was firing for Terry Hodgson on the N2 tank when they were filming the Scotch Flyer scene where the children ask "Why's it going so slowly Mr. Perks?" Those kids weren't joking for we seemed to spend hours sitting around in the sun at Oakworth station while the film crew tried to made up their minds what they wanted to do next.

The frantic inactivity continued until finally, someone produced a camera and some publicity shots were taken of the cast in front of the engine. After this we propelled the train around the bend clear of the station and awaited instructions. Sadly, none were forthcoming so the sunbathing resumed. When we were finally called to do the run through the station, everyone seemed satisfied so we returned to Oxenhope – and more sunshine. It's all go is this filming lark.

LEFT – Derrick on the footplate of No. 957
Photo: D. Begg Collection

Arrival of the Russian

I was firing the Manchester Ship Canal tank engine No. 67 which was on the train bringing 'The Shabby Russian' to Oakworth in the middle of rainstorm. It was actually a scorching hot day so the impressive deluge was ably provided by the local fire brigade, who couldn't resist turning the hose in our direction for a quick blast across the footplate. As Mr Perks said, "Don't mind the rain it's only a shower".

As we stood in the platform, the left hand clack valve was blowing back and, just as the crew commenced filming, there was a resounding clang as my driver hit the clack valve with a coal hammer. We were not too popular.

The Paper Chase

I was firing for Terry Hodgson on No. 957 'The Green Dragon' during the paperchase scene. Having collected our coaches we proceeded to the south end of Mytholmes tunnel where we sat quite a while awaiting instructions. A filming chap eventually came along and told us they were ready and could we make as much smoke as possible to give the impression Mytholmes tunnel was much longer than it actually is. As we were on a falling gradient, all Terry had to do was release the brake. With no steam on, the damper shut, the firehole door shut, the blower off, and a few well placed shovels of coal, we were making plenty of smoke. All I can remember as we roared through the tunnel in a cloud of clag was the lights as we passed the film crew. We stopped shortly afterwards on Mytholmes viaduct and looked back to see smoke pouring out of the tunnel mouth down to about two feet off the ground. A few minutes later people started to appear out of the smoke amid a lot of coughing and gasping for air. We had clearly done our job well .....

Terry and I then discussed whether to go down to Keighley for water or just propel the stock back to Haworth. It was decided to do the latter so I made up the fire and got the engine ready. With the guard waving us on we proceeded up the hill. Suddenly the guard gave us a rather frantic stop signal, so I shouted across to Terry who immediately put the brake on and we ground to a halt a couple of coach lengths later. Crouched in the cess was one of the film crew's electricians looking rather alarmed. He had in his hands two ends of a rather long cable. It appears the cable has been run across the railway without anyone informing us and our unhappy film man was now the proud owner of two long lengths of cable and one of just 4 foot 8½ inches.

When I informed Terry Hodgson of the fact, he took one puff on his fag and said, "---- 'em" and opened the regulator. I could do nothing but shrug my shoulders as I looked down on the poor chap as we passed.

ABOVE – Left to right: Terry Hodgson, Fred Crowther and Derrick Begg on the footplate of locomotive No. 957 at Oxenhope – Photo: Richard Greenwood

Pannier Tank to Shipley
For some of the scenes, the locomotives had to be turned to face the other way and this usually necessitated a trip to Shipley triangle. On one occasion I rode in the cab of the pannier tank L89 while a B.R. Class 25 diesel hauled it along the main line to Shipley and back. It was quite an exciting trip and I think the BR crew were on bonus.

The rest of my time during the filming was spent cleaning and repairing the engines at Haworth. Unfortunately I did not see the end of the filming as my employers, Mobil Oil, required me back at sea. '

"The trees are walking down the bank" _____

Creating the famous landslide scene caused more than a few headaches, not least for the driver of the 'Green Dragon' locomotive which set it off - MIKE GOODALL

ABOVE – Mr. Goodall takes 'The Green Dragon' past the landslide site. The channels in which the trees slide down the bank are clearly visible – Photo: Roger Bastin

Monday 8th June 1970 was already sweltering when I arrived in Haworth yard at 6am to get the steam locomotive No. 957 'The Green Dragon' ready for the day's filming. We were doing the landslide scene – the bit where the train charges through a cutting which then falls down. The yard was deserted and the loco which was supposed to set off at 8am, was not even lit up. This came as no great surprise as despite their elaborate plans, or 'shooting schedules' as I believe they call them, the film people often seemed to ignore everything and apparently make it up as they went along. To be fair, with actors having other commitments, getting them all together must have been a task to try the patience of Job. Thus when I found 957 standing idle, I assumed that there might have been an overnight change of plan. On the other hand, last minute changes of plan lead to many late-night-cum-early-morning shunts and perhaps the rest of the crew had just 'crashed out' through sheer exhaustion. To be on the safe side, I lit a fire in No. 957 and proceeded to get it ready. For two hours I had the place to myself, then at last came a sign that there was alternative life in Haworth. A gentleman approached and enquired if the train would be ready at the landslide site by 8.30am. I had to admire his sense of humour, for the chances of No. 957 even being on the boil by that hour were extremely remote. Sadly he was not joking and he went off to wait expectantly, if pointlessly, for the train at Mytholmes.

Enter Railway Chairman and film company 'Technical Consultant' Bob Cryer. Could I take the camera crew down to the site with D226? Err, no I could not. We had a golden rule that steam locomotives must not be left unattended if they were lit up, and I was the only person around. Bob vanished in the direction of the sleeping car to find the rest of the crew who, as I expected, had been shunting into the early hours. With assistance now at hand, I ferried the camera crew to the tunnel mouth.

Returning to Haworth, it was obvious that No. 957 was reluctant to make steam. With D226 hooked on to the front, the idle beast was dragged up and down the loop and persuaded to join the party. At last we were all ready and, some two hours behind schedule, we arrived on location. Having taken part in other filming epics, I was not entirely surprised to learn that nobody had really missed us. Had I not had the presence of mind to equip myself with 'The Times' the following hour or so would have been extremely boring, the only activity being that of the fibreglass tree sliding ponderously up and down the side of the cutting to the great amusement of the many locals who had gathered to watch the proceedings.

ABOVE – The famous fibreglass tree is securely lashed in place awaiting its starring role as members of the film crew are ferried around on the diesel railbus – Photo: Brian Baker

Time passed slowly by - then action at last. A gentleman bearing a walkie-talkie climbed on board. Could we run up past the cameras? 'Certainly – how fast shall we go?' 'As fast as you can' he replied. Unfortunately with the best part of 100 tons in tow, No. 957 did not want to go at all, at least not up the hill, which seemed a pity because that was where the cameras were situated. After several futile attempts to go forwards, I decided to set off back into Oakworth station. Off the curve, we stood a better chance of getting to grips with the rails.

With the chance to take a bit of a run at it, No. 957 now charged round Mytholmes curve and shot through the tunnel at a steady 30mph in full gear and second valve. Once clear of the tunnel, I stopped its gallop only for the walkie-talkie to burst into life. Could we do it again? Certainly – and again and again.

Over the next hour we made several 'flat out' runs using a boiler-full of water on each occasion. By the time lunch was taken, the tank was nearly empty so I asked the gentleman with the walkie-talkie what we were going to do afterwards. If we were to continue with the action, I would take the opportunity to go for water. The ether crackled and after a few moments he confirmed that we had finished filming. The afternoon was to be taken up with sound effects well away from the tunnel.

ABOVE – Setting up the landslide at Mytholmes cutting – Photo: Brian Baker

Lunch was a pleasant and unhurried affair taken in the yard of Vale Mill at Oakworth. No. 957 simmered under the trees South of the level crossing as we awaited our marching orders. Eventually the walkie-talkie returned – could we run past the cameras again? 'Pardon, I thought we had done that lot'. 'Oh no', came the reply, 'We want some more footage'. My language at this point would have got the blue pencil in the 'Bargees Weekly Chronicle'. We did a run, and then another. After the second run they asked for a third, but backing down towards Oakworth station we thought "What about water?" The injectors answered the question. One coughed, spluttered and failed to restart, followed almost immediately by the other. Now with a heavy train, an empty tank, a half empty boiler, and the nearest water supply two steeply climbing miles away, one can do one of two things: ditch the train and run like hell to the water supply, or throw the fire out. We opted for the former course of action.

As we uncoupled the train in Oakworth station, the walkie-talkie man became very agitated. Could we not wait a few minutes whilst he found out what was happening? 'No, we could not', came the stern reply. We had run right out of minutes and what was happening was quite simple; we were going for water, with or without him. He got off and we departed. No. 957 fairly galloped towards Mytholmes where a number of people were disporting themselves around the tunnel mouth – that mobile tree again. A series of frantic crows on the whistle persuaded them to clear the track. Through the tunnel, past Haworth to the welcoming sight of Oxenhope and the water tank.

ABOVE – The children race to save the train from disaster – Photo: Robin Higgins

With the boiler now empty, the burning question was would No. 957's often troublesome lifting injectors start again? They had been on their best behaviour all day but a spell of idleness in the scorching heat of the afternoon was just the sort of thing to make them play silly so-and-sos. With the water descending full bore into the tank, I tried the right hand injector. No cough, no splutter – it sang away as if it had never been off. The left hand one followed suit.

With the boiler and tank filled, we set off back. As we approached Haworth, someone suggested a wash in the porter's room. After a day of heat and grime, this sounded like a good idea. Then someone else suggested an ice cream so we paused on the platform. Having removed the encrusted dirt, and with an ice lolly clutched firmly in my hand, I emerged from the porters room and bumped into irate Railway boss Brian Baker. The film company were paying us good money and here we were idling our time away when we should have been filming. Gesticulating fiercely with my ice lolly, I pointed out that if the so-and-so film company could not make their so-and-so minds up as to what they were doing from one side of the lunch break to the other, then hard so-and-so lines. What was more, if Lionel Jeffries had any complaints, I would be only too pleased to tell him so to his face. Brian departed, and so did I.

Passing Mytholmes, guess what they were playing with? Correct in one – the mobile tree was still sliding up and down the side of the cutting. We reached Oakworth station and you would have thought that we had never left the place. Train? What train? Who wants a train anyway? We spent a pleasant hour or three in the sunshine of a perfect June afternoon and then, with the imitation tree securely parked for the night, made our way back to Haworth yard.

ABOVE – The fibreglass tree is erected above the timber retaining wall – Photo: Robin Lush

ABOVE – 'The trees are walking down the bank' – Photo: Robin Lush

BELOW - A miniature camera was fitted inside a fibreglass boulder to secure action shots during the landslide scene. This anonymous and rather faded newspaper cutting shows one of the crew putting the 'boulder' in place at the top of the cutting.

"The hound in the red jersey" _____

HOWARD MAIS recalls his role as an 'extra' in the paperchase scene. This article first appeared in 'Down Your Way' magazine and is reprinted here with their kind permission.

In March 1970 the tedium of preparing for ordinary level examinations for the fifth form at Roundhay Grammar School in Leeds was lifted when our English Language teacher, John Shuttleworth, told us that extras were being sought for the forthcoming filming of 'The Railway Children' in and around Oakworth and that if anyone was interested they should let him know and attend a selection meeting after school. To this day I do not know why our school and form were chosen for this, but it did cause a certain amount of envy among friends.

Having keenly put my name forward I attended the meeting a couple of evenings later. The Director and Screenplay Writer, former comedy actor Lionel Jeffries, came to the school with one of his colleagues and we were told that they were looking to choose "Twenty lads of assorted shapes and sizes" to participate in the paper chase scenes.

ABOVE – Lionel Jeffries and cast above Mytholmes tunnel – Photo: Roger Bastin

Being 6 feet 6 inches tall I had no trouble in meeting the assorted shape and size criteria and so some weeks later myself and nineteen class mates found ourselves being picked up by coach from near the school in the early morning. We did not go straight to Oakworth but instead diverted to the Merrion Centre Hotel to pick up others who would be involved with the film. These people turned out mainly to be extras as well, but from within the acting profession. Of course the stars of the film were transported in chauffeur-driven cars and were not expected to share a coach with twenty schoolboys.

When we arrived at Oakworth our changing rooms turned out, most appropriately, to be the compartments of an unused railway carriage. We were all provided with a set of black or white knickerbockers and a multi-coloured rugby shirt and soon got ourselves changed and ready.

The experience was great fun and we spent, if I recall correctly, three full days in Oakworth over a couple of weeks. The weather on all the days we were there was fine and sunny and I presume that those days had been chosen on the basis of reliable weather forecasting. Much of our time, though, was spent watching other scenes being filmed, including the famous avalanche scene, rather than being filmed ourselves.

ABOVE – The children try to rescue the injured runner – Photo: Canal + Image UK Ltd.

Our main piece of action was when the paper chase went through a tunnel. One of the smaller lads among us, Ozzie, was chosen to be the hare and as he had a line to say in the film he was paid twice as much as the rest of us. Very soon we were filming the scene in which Ozzie spoke his line of "Let me pass please" to the Railway Children before he entered the tunnel. The rest of us watched a number of takes before it was our turn to be filmed running down the railway banking past the Railway Children and disappearing into the tunnel. Again there were a number of takes and none of us really knew what was making one take acceptable and others not. We were then able to watch the filming of the actor who was running well behind the rest of us entering the tunnel. In the story he fell and broke his leg in the tunnel only to be saved by the Railway Children before a train could arrive and run him over.

We didn't have to run through the tunnel but our next scene involved queuing up to run out of it and up the steep banking. Again there were a number of takes and for the last one we were asked to collapse with exhaustion when part way up the banking. We all then displayed what we naively believed to be our superb acting talents by falling on the banking, usually as if shot by an unseen sniper. With the benefit of hindsight it was realised that this had been purely for the amusement of the film crew who probably never even set the cameras rolling. There were certainly no dying paper chasers to be seen when the film eventually came out.

We then had to do some long distance running shots through the village and across the countryside, crossing fields and leaping over dry stone walls. One of our classmates, Ox, didn't leap high enough and partly demolished one of the walls to great amusement but this comedy moment did not make the final cut.

LEFT – With the train due at any time, runner Jim lies trapped inside the tunnel with a broken leg

Photo: Canal + Image UK Ltd.

The last thing I recall us doing was some sound recording. We were assembled on the platform of Oakworth station and asked to run on the spot. We were told that when we were pointed to we should say something that we might spontaneously have said whilst running in a real paper chase. However the kind of things we were prone to say as 1970s schoolboys were not always representative of what Edwardian schoolboys might have said in the same circumstances. Nevertheless some of the more acceptable comments can be heard during the tunnel scenes.

Nineteen of us were paid £5 per day for our efforts whilst Ozzie received £10 per day. This was good and very welcome money for schoolboys in 1970. We were also fed for free from the mobile catering units. However to this day I do regret not having done a deal for royalties in the light of how often the film is screened, especially as that proved to be the beginning and end of my acting career.

When the film was released we all went to the cinema on the opening night to see it. To say we had spent three days on set it was surprising how short the scenes we appeared in turned out to be. We were on screen for a total of about fifty seconds out of the film's running time of approximately one and three quarter hours. As a consequence I do not think that every one of the twenty of us actually appeared on screen. I was pleased to see that I did but these days very few people can recognise me unless I point myself out, such have been the ravages of time on my physique and appearance.

"Stop, Stop"

The scene where Bobbie waved her Red Flannel Petticoat to stop the train from running into the landslide was filmed in reverse. If you watch the film closely you can actually see the smoke going back into the locomotive's chimney. This was one of the few scenes where the track was clearly visible so the concrete sleepers were boxed in to make them look like wooden sleepers.

Photos - Top: Canal + Image UK Ltd   Bottom: Brian Baker

The Old Gentleman's Saloon

The 'Old Gentleman's Saloon' from 'The Railway Children' has a history of railway use stretching back over 140 years, as owner CHRIS LAWSON recalls.

ABOVE – The saloon basks in the sun at Oxenhope station – Photo: Chris Lawson

It was originally built in 1871 as a 4 wheeled smoking saloon for the Stockton and Darlington Railway (S&DR). Three years previously, Parliament had passed legislation requiring the railways to provide separate smoking accommodation for their passengers. In response, the S&DR ordered the construction of two smoking saloons at Darlington, of which this was one, for use on their long distance routes, mainly over Stainmore to Tebay and Penrith. Although taken over by the North Eastern Railway (NER) in 1863, the S&DR operated as a separate entity until 1876, when all rolling stock was incorporated into the NER. At this time the Saloon became No 1661 under the NER numbering system.

It continued in use as a smoking saloon until the early 1880s, when it was put on to a 6 wheeled frame and converted to become the Inspection Saloon for the Locomotive Superintendent of the NER. It was based at Gateshead Locomotive Works and paired with locomotive No 66 'Aerolite'. As such it was used by the Locomotive Superintendent as his private train to carry out inspections of the premises – locomotive works, engine sheds, carriage and wagon works – and staff for whom he was responsible across the NER area. The precise date of its conversion is not clear, but it is likely to have been used by Edward Fletcher and Archibald McDonnell and certainly by the Worsdell brothers, TW and then Wilson.

1900 saw its use on a Royal Train from York to Newcastle, conveying the then Prince (later Edward VII) and Princess of Wales for the laying of the foundation stone of what is now the Royal Victoria Infirmary.

By 1904, Wilson Worsdell had decided that the Locomotive Superintendent should in future be known as the Chief Mechanical Engineer (CME) and that his Inspection Saloon should be upgraded. It was therefore lengthened and placed on a bogie frame, providing a saloon seating 15 with armchairs and a meeting table, a toilet, guard/stewards compartment with wine rack and cool box, and a kitchen with crockery and cutlery cupboards – a self contained office on wheels. This internal layout is retained in the Saloon to the present day.

On Worsdell's retirement in 1910, the Saloon was moved to Darlington North Road, along with 'Aerolite' and the NER Dynamometer Car, and was re-allocated to the Assistant CME, A.C. Stamer. He continued to use it, through the Grouping and the formation of the London and North Eastern Railway (LNER) in 1923 when it was renumbered 21661, until his retirement at the end of 1933. At that time, 'Aerolite' was withdrawn for preservation and can now be seen at the National Railway Museum in York, and the Saloon was moved to York Carriage Works where, in 1934, it was converted to its present external condition with large picture windows.

ABOVE – Awaiting passengers for the Cream Tea Specials - Photo: Chris Lawson

Subsequently it was first used by Edward Thompson and then by Arthur Peppercorn as their Inspection Saloon while they were based at Darlington, before being moved to York on the nationalisation of the railways at the beginning of 1948. Here it became the Inspection Saloon for the Chief Regional Officer of the new North Eastern Region of British Railways (BR) and was renumbered E902179E. It was finally transferred to the Signal and Telecommunications (S&T) Department at York in the early 1950s, where it was used by the S&T Engineer, Arthur Wigram, for his inspections of signalling schemes across the Region.

By March 1969, the Saloon was deemed surplus to requirements and was purchased privately by the late John Dawson in March 1969 from BR for £500. It was moved to the preserved and newly reopened Keighley and Worth Valley Railway (KWVR) in West Yorkshire in May and, in 1970, became the 'Old Gentleman's Saloon' in 'The Railway Children' film, in which William Mervyn played the 'Old Gentleman'.

Normally based on the KWVR, as an ex-S&DR vehicle it was exhibited at the Stockton and Darlington Railway 150 Anniversary celebrations at Shildon in August 1975. For this it was put through Doncaster BR Engineering Works where it was restored to the varnished teak livery in which it can be seen today. From May to October 1977 the Saloon was on hire to the Derwent Valley Light Railway at York for the operation of a steam hauled passenger service on this otherwise freight only line. The Saloon has also been on display at the National Railway Museum in York on three separate occasions, and in 1991 visited the North Yorkshire Moors Railway as part of the celebrations of the 25th Anniversary of the North Eastern Locomotive Preservation Group.

Now owned privately by Chris Lawson, it is normally kept in the Carriage Shed at Oxenhope, but it does see use on filming assignments, special trains (including a visit to the Railway by the Duke of Kent in 2008), and on Vintage Train weekends during the summer when cream teas are served on board to passengers who have booked for a round trip on the line. In 2010 the Saloon played a major role in the celebrations, both on the KWVR and elsewhere, to mark the 40th Anniversary of the making of 'The Railway Children' film.

ABOVE – The saloon passes the film crew near Mytholmes tunnel – Photo: Bill Black

"Excellent Hastwell"

Most people probably didn't even notice him as the Butler in the Old Gentleman's Saloon but Ken Hastwell, a former cinema projectionist from Leeds, had an impressive list of acting roles on his CV. Apart from his brief appearance in 'The Railway Children' Ken appeared as an extra in Coronation Street, Heartbeat, Only Fools and Horses, Emmerdale Farm, Open All Hours, Ripping Yarns, Sherlock Holmes, The Flaxton Boys, Taggart, All Creatures Great & Small and Yanks.

Ken also came to the Railway in 1979 as an extra in the famous comedy series 'Last of the Summer Wine'. In the episode 'Full Steam Behind' he played a Mayor who was officiating at Oakworth station during the re-opening of the line. Obviously Compo (Bill Owen), Foggy (Brian Wilde) and Clegg (Peter Sallis) ensured that chaos ensued. This episode of the long running series was reputedly a firm favourite with actor Peter Sallis.

Ken often appeared in the series as Compo's stunt double and recalled, "If you saw a pair of wellies sticking up in the air or Compo flying over a wall or off a pushbike, that was probably me".

During 2010 we were delighted to welcome Ken as a customer on board the Old Gentleman's Saloon where he was served Cream Tea by your scribe dressed in full butler regalia. He clearly had fond memories of working on 'The Railway Children', telling us, "I spent five weeks at the Railway playing a waiter who served some wine to William Mervyn on board the Saloon. It took a while to get used to the movement of the train while pouring the wine but it was a most enjoyable time".

Ken was in his mid eighties when he sadly passed away early in 2012. All of the photographs on this page are from his personal collection.

"Daddy, my Daddy"

More than forty years have passed since Jenny Agutter uttered those immortal words, so perhaps it is time to lift the lid off the real events of 1970 – MIKE GOODALL reveals all.

The final scheduled day's shooting was for the 'Daddy, My Daddy' scene where father returned home from prison – and it was a complete farce. Mind you, after five weeks of swapping and changing, it was perhaps inevitable that the film crew would end up with the wrong train.

ABOVE – The memorable reunion scene at Oakworth station - Photo: Canal + Image UK Ltd.

The film trains consisted of 'The Green Dragon', the 'Scotch Flyer', the 'Old Gentleman's Train' and the local train which apparently came from Wakefield. The latter consisted of Manchester Ship Canal 0-6-0T No. 67 and a selection of four or six wheeled coaches and had been specially provided with a continuous pipe beneath the footboards from which copious amounts of steam could blow across the platform. When Daddy returned from his unfortunate encounter with the prison service, the idea was that he should emerge from the midst of this steam into the arms of his unbelieving elder daughter. Unfortunately they asked for - and got - the Old Gentleman's Train. Not only was there no leaky pipe from which steam could issue profusely, but the Old Gentleman's engine, Pannier L89, did not even have steam heating equipment.

When the mistake was discovered, several things happened almost simultaneously. One group of people, no doubt with an eye on their future employment in the film industry, descended on the unfortunate Lionel Jeffries to let him know it wasn't their fault. Others, a little less sanguine, aired their superior knowledge by informing all and sundry that they knew it was the wrong train all along.

A special effects man attempted to salvage the day by sticking a long rubber hose on one of L89's injector overflow pipes and laying it under the train. Steam did blow out over the platform until the injector overheated and burst a joint. Steam then blew all over L89. A random selection of expletives persuaded the man that his suggestion to repeat the experiment with the remaining injector did not meet with the approval of the train crew.

LEFT – Mike Goodall's charge, pannier tank L89, which got the film crews all steamed up during filming at Oakworth

Photo: Robin Higgins

Considering that he was the Director, Lionel Jeffries appeared to take the whole thing most calmly. He had contingency funds for 'hidden extras' so could we come back the following day with the correct train? The following day we turned up at Oakworth with the correct train plus L89. Two engines with only one crew; highly irregular, so could we have double pay? I regret to say we are still waiting for this. With L89 dumped in the back siding, we did the emotional arrival, complete with steam clouds. The train was then swapped for L89. During the previous day's debacle, Lionel had thought up an extra shot to heighten the drama of the landslide scene. Fasten a camera to the leading steps and let it run as the engine bore down on the petticoat-waving children. With the wheel revolving ponderously in front of the lens, we trundled off towards Damems for this last shot.

Additional footage was taken through the cab window and then it was back to Oakworth. Lionel Jeffries made a little speech thanking everybody and told them to 'break the set', by which we assumed that the whole affair was over. The film people started to load their equipment while we whilst we hooked up No. 67 and its train. The excitement over, we made our leisurely way back to Oxenhope to dump the train and water the engines. When we eventually arrived back in Haworth yard, we were accosted by some none-too-pleased individuals with a large pantechnicon. It was the costume department. For some obscure reason we had been fitted into some period garments and now they wanted them back. With the rest of the film crew half way to London by now, they were still stuck in the back of beyond awaiting the return of a train crew who could see no reason to rush and who, if the truth were known, had completely forgotten that they were wearing somebody else's trousers.

With their departure, Sleepy Hollow returned to normal. True, a camera crew did come back for some additional train shots, but that, as far as we were concerned, was the end of 'The Railway Children'. Or so we thought ....

"Conversationalising with the junior public" _

KWVR volunteer DAVID PEARSON recalls his days as a short-trousered school boy and how he played a part in the famous 'Daddy, My Daddy' reunion scene.

I was 15 when 'The Railway Children' was filmed and recall it very well indeed. I was still at school (St. Bede's in Bradford) and ached every day to get to the Railway so that I could see what was going on. It must have been filmed some time round the holidays (Easter I think) as I know that I spent a lot of full days at Oakworth and did all sorts of odd jobs around the place. One thing which sticks clearly in my memory is Lionel Jeffries calling out numbers when the train stopped with Mother arriving from Wakefield. Each number was a passenger in one of the Metropolitan Coaches and they popped out according to the numbers; it looks a bit false on the finished film and staged, and that's why.

ABOVE - Another shot is lined up at Oakworth station - Photo: Brian Baker

The landslide was fun. It had to be cleared up for the following weekend's services and could only be done once; it was a bit like watching 'The Bridge on the River Kwai', but it worked. We had the fake tree for years afterwards in Oakworth Yard and you can still see the place where the wall above Norman Feather's coal pile was demolished and rebuilt to allow Peter to come and steal the coal to keep Mother warm.

There was quite a lot of movement between Keighley and Shipley to turn locomotives on the triangle. It was very easy to arrange in those days. 957 was sent there a couple of times and somewhere I have some photographs of her standing in platform 3, in full GN & SR livery after having been returned by BR from such a trip. I never thought how much she would thirty years later, dominate my life.

On one very memorable occasion, we were hanging around Oakworth and William Mervyn (right) became bored. He shouted to Lionel Jeffries (below) something like "Do you need this bloody train Lionel?" to which he received a negative reply. I can recall the confidence and incredulity that I experienced as the incomparable Mervyn (he was already a hero to me from his role as the Bishop in 'All Gas and Gaiters') ordered the pannier tank and Old Gentleman's saloon full of us 'helpers' to Haworth where we decamped to the Royal Oak, Bill Mervyn in costume rapping on the bar and ordering "Two gallons for my Railway friends, landlord if you please". It's a daft tale I know, but one which made a most profound impression upon a very impressionable youth.

I suppose one of the daftest things I ever did was to find a script for the film, full of actor's annotations which had been thrown away in a bin in Haworth Yard, look at it and throw it away in turn; it would probably have been worth a bob or two now. It came from a row of coaches in the Yard (there was no New Shed there then) which were used as a wardrobe and dressing rooms for the extras.

The Hares and Hounds were posh kids from Roundhay Grammar School, which was a sequence I recall took a few days to film. For a time it looked as if the film crew would round up any handy adolescents from the valley to fill the extras' parts, but our hopes were dashed.

In the event, I did get a role. If you look at the very end of the film, as Father arrives and steam clears, you can see me closing the level crossing gates. Phil Slack, the then Oakworth Stationmaster ought to have done it, but he was away for some reason so I got my first ever paid job and the only cash that to this day, I have ever had as a result of my involvement in the Railway. A fiver was a fortune in those days and I recall I bought a book with it.

The scenes of the train heading towards the landslide were done much later, when the weather was very hot and it was our school summer holiday. Some might find it difficult to believe, but I cleaned the pannier tank on those days and got the odd footplate ride as a result. It was my first since BR days, when I had a run on an Ivatt tank on the Push & Pull service, so it really meant a lot to me.

It's all a lifetime away now but perhaps one day we will be able to do something like it all over again. One thing's for sure, I'll certainly never forget it all.

Photos: Robin Lush

Costume and Make Up _____

The film company set up a site office and costume department in some railway carriages in Haworth Yard. Long standing KWVR volunteer KEN ROBERTS was there and recalls many incidents which took place in 'his' carriages

I had a few days off in May 1970 during the filming of 'The Railway Children', and upon entering Haworth Yard I noticed several coaches being set down into the old No. 4 road. I later learnt that they were to become the on-site headquarters of the film company. From memory, among the coaches were the Chatham brake, Pullmans 84 and 'Zena', the latter now forming part of the Orient Express rake. A day or so later I noticed that the local Electric Board had fixed up heating and lighting in all these coaches. That same evening, a few of us had a sneaky look inside them ..... wow. Edwardian clothes were hanging up from racks and spread all over the place. A couple of lads put on strange headgear such as bobbies helmets, pith helmets and pill box hats. A security firm called Wideawake was apparently employed to keep guard of things but was clearly not wide awake when the aforementioned capers took place. Wideawake's alsation dog had a sort of silent bark and could hardly walk. Photos: Brian Baker (above), Roger Bastin (below)

The following day we again ventured into the coaches to find more interesting things. Inside the Chatham was a lady operating a huge washing machine. She told us that she went out East to do any washing during 'Lawrence of Arabia'. "By gum" said one of the lads, "I'll bet that machine got bunged up with sand". The lady did not think the remark was funny and said "Don't think I'm going to wash your lot's dirty overalls".

Going into the Pullman cars and ploughing through Edwardian frocks and other frilly things, tail coats etc, we went into 'Zena' which, being a first class Pullman, had private cubicles at each end of the car. One was for Dinah Sheridan and the other was for Bernard Cribbins. In the centre of this car was a large board on which were written the names of the cast, the Producer and Director, and the Technical Director the late Bob Cryer. Now Bob was a movie buff and so got his name, at last, on the screen.

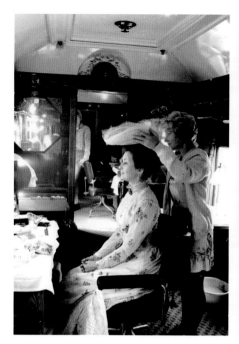

LEFT – Hairdresser Helen Lennox attends to Dinah Sheridan in the elegant surroundings of the first class Pullman Car 'Zena' – Photo: Canal + Image UK Ltd.

RIGHT – Sally Thomsett (Phyliss) receives attention from the Make-up Department in Haworth Yard – Photo: Robin Higgins

Some members of the Railway were asked to do fire-watching duties for a wage of £4 per person per night. That was good money in those days but the Railway's Council had decided that any member doing this work should hand back all, or at least 50%, of those earnings. £4 was also the amount paid to the lads from a school in Leeds for their part in the paper chase scene. On giving the lads the money, the School Master remarked, "That is the easiest money you will ever earn in your lives".

Down at Oakworth, one of the coach's droplight straps broke. Asking one of the film staff where I might get some strong thread, I was directed towards the Wardrobe Department. "See those fancy boys over there ..... that is the wardrobe department".

There was a short break in filming over the Whit weekend and the weather was nice and warm. One scene at Oakworth demanded a wet platform so out came the local fire brigade to provide torrential rain on demand. Chatting to Jenny Agutter at Oakworth, I asked if she had gone South with the rest of the crowd over Whit. I thought I heard her say "No, I have been to see my parents in St Helens". Methinks this lass is no snob.

To many of the onlookers, the star of the whole event was the film's Director Lionel Jeffries. Already well known as an actor, 'The Railway Children' was his first stint as Director. He usually arrived on the set at about 7am with a very big red scarf around him and an after-shave with an aroma not unlike The Famous Grouse or Arthur Bell – a splendid chap.

KWVR volunteer Mike Goodall recalls the difficulties that the costume department must have faced when confronted by persons who possess what are, to say the least, oversize figures. For the final scenes of the film, two drivers were teamed together on the footplate. One was modest in structure, the other rather generous. They were required to be in costume even though, as it turned out, they never appeared in front of the camera. The costume department searched their wardrobes for suitable garments and whilst they had some measure of success with the more proportionate 'driver' they had to admit defeat on the outsize 'fireman'. The latter, with a pair of trousers several sizes too small around the middle, finished up looking more like a robust participant at Sadlers Wells than anything connected with a railway. In imminent danger of serious injury should he so much as attempt to pick up a shovel, the 'fireman' quickly changed roles with the 'driver'.

One of the hairdressers working on the film was Helen Lennox, who is seen here on set with Jenny Agutter. Helen's daughter, Victoria Evans, has fond memories of her late mother and recalls:

"Helen had a long and happy career in the British film industry. She was a wonderful hairdresser and a bright and shining human being. She worked on many films spanning her thirty year career. Rocky Horror show, James Bond. Chitty Chitty Bang Bang and Star Wars, and with legends such as Mick Jagger, Elizabeth Taylor, Bette Davis, Joan Collins, and Anthony Quinn, to name a few. The Railway Children was for her a happy time. She mentioned it often with a fondness. It holds a dear place in my heart too as decades later Bernard Cribbins who was a dear friend became my godfather."

Photo: Robin Higgins

The Brass Band

In the words of the much missed Eric Morecambe, "All the right notes, but not necessarily in the right order".

Members of the Haworth Brass Band put in a memorable performance during the presentation scene at Oakworth while under the baton of their increasingly frustrated bandmaster, played by the actor David Lodge.

Photo: Haworth Band

Haworth Brass Band continues to flourish and when additional scenes were required for the remastered DVD version of the film in 2010, we were delighted to welcome back some of the band members who took part in the 1970 filming – Photo: Jim Shipley

Sitting In The Sun _____

While the extras stood around waiting for their moment of fame, all of the leading players had personalised chairs where they could relax and discuss the next scene in the glorious summer weather of 1970. Nobody went hungry during filming thanks to the excellent on-site catering facilities laid on by the film company.

ABOVE – Bernard Cribbins spends time "Conversationalising with the junior public" at Oakworth station – Photo: Peter Eastham

ABOVE – Lionel Jeffries and members of the cast relax in between takes at Oakworth station
Photo: N.R. Knight

BELOW – The film crew and actors take advantage of the glorious summer sun at Oakworth
station – Photo: Robin Higgins

"There's going to be a Paperchase"

Now a Series Producer for BBC television, MARSHALL CORWIN recalls how he landed his first media role as a boy runner in the paper chase scene.

I was always into drama and steam engines from an early age and was so excited to learn that Lionel Jeffries and his team would be visiting my school, Roundhay Grammar in Leeds, to choose the boys for the paper chase sequence. Unfortunately, it quickly emerged that the visit would coincide with the dress rehearsal of our school play, Shakespeare's Coriolanus, in which I was playing a Roman Senator. During a break in the rehearsal I ran round to the classroom where the casting was in full swing. My appearance at the door, wearing nothing but a rather short Roman toga, interrupted proceedings and caused quite a stir. Fortunately Lionel saw the funny side, immediately turning to one of his colleagues saying, "Oh, well we must have him."

ABOVE – The runners enter Mytholmes tunnel – Photo: Canal + Image UK Ltd.

Everything about the filming was memorable: the crazy early start hearing the dawn chorus for the first time; the gorgeous little station littered with movie stars; the fascinating business and paraphernalia of filming; from the antiquated costumes to the scene after scene in the sensational countryside where the sun always shone. And through it all I was desperately trying to figure a way to catch the eye of one of the production team, in the forlorn and faintly ludicrous hope they would magically realise just how remarkably talented this scrawny fifteen year old extra was and instantly offer me a long-term job.

Some years later I decided to try to join the BBC, and I have in fact spent my entire career in the media in a variety of dream jobs. By happy coincidence the last decade has been particularly fulfilling, taking young people of similar age on their own magical journeys to far-flung parts of the world for a TV series I created called 'Serious Explorers', seen on children's BBC.

"Most extraordinary indeed"

KWVR steam driver, NICK HELLEWELL, recalls his starring role with the Old Gentleman's Train, and how Lionel Jeffries' handkerchief saved the day.

One of those perfect early summer mornings in 1970 found us chuffing gently up towards Oxenhope, with the 'put-put' of the vacuum pump on the pannier tank prompting my driver, Bob Phizackerley, to remark that we might have been anywhere on the Western Region of British Railways with a branch train to somewhere rural.

Our duty was to do whatever director Lionel Jeffries (pictured left) asked of us with this, the Old Gentleman's Train. Our pannier tank No. L89 of 1929 vintage, would have to come bursting out of Mytholmes tunnel an endless number of times with her train before the day was over. We had a man with a walkie-talkie on the footplate to give instructions like, "Stop", "Go", "Faster", "Slower", and also "Can you make it stay quiet now?" This latter request coming only minutes after him telling us, "We shall need a high speed run with plenty of noise and steam as soon as you can, driver".

We devoted a whole morning to this activity, watching the three children wave at us from the lineside fence. We also had to keep an eye on a man who ran along the line with a flag held aloft, allegedly at a similar speed to our own. We were fortunate in that the Old Gentleman (alias the late William Mervyn), sitting in the rear saloon carriage, seemed to have a thirst that coincided with our pannier - so with an influential word to Mr Jeffries, we were released to Oxenhope where water was taken. There then followed a rapid descent to Haworth where everyone (except me) followed the Old Gentleman's invitation to the Royal Oak. I loyally stuck to my post lest the pannier tank should have any silly ideas of her own. We shortly backed down to Mytholmes where, in true film company fashion, a feast had been laid out on tables above the tunnel.

The afternoon continued much as the morning, but here lies my ultimate claim to fame. When the time came to shoot the final run-past where all and sundry wave at the children to indicate their pleasure at the release of their father from prison, my handkerchief, after many hours on the footplate, proved to be inadequately white for waving. Lionel Jeffries loaned me his and that part of the film was in the can. – Photo: KWVR

Lights, Camera, Action _____

Hollywood comes to Haworth? – It certainly seemed that way during the glorious summer months of 1970 when the Railway was turned into a huge film set and railway volunteers worked alongside the technicians and actors to bring Edith Nesbit's famous story to the silver screen.

ABOVE – Peter Bromilow (Doctor Forrest), Gary Warren (Peter), and Sally Thomsett (Phyliss) get lined up for another shot at Oakworth station – Photo: Peter Eastham

ABOVE – Director Lionel Jeffries and crew on Oakworth platform – Photo: Robin Higgins

BELOW – The film crew fix electrical cables between the coaches - Photo: Martin Welch

ABOVE – The crew discuss the next shot near Mytholmes tunnel – Photo: Roger Bastin

BELOW – Filming the return of 'The Shabby Russian' – Photo: Nigel Hunt

ABOVE – Young actress Jenny Agutter gazes admiringly at Dinah Sheridan during preparation for filming of 'The End' scene at Ebor Lane near Haworth - Photo: Canal + Image UK Ltd.

"Perks must be about it" _____

Bernard Cribbins and his character of Mr Perks are now forever linked with Oakworth, as former Station Master JIM SHIPLEY recalls.

Bernard Cribbins was already a well known and respected comedy actor when he played the part of Perks the Porter in 'The Railway Children'. Having made a name for himself on the London stage, he went on to appear in numerous films including Tommy the Toreador (with Tommy Steele), Two Way Stretch and The Wrong Arm of the Law (with Peter Sellers), and three Carry On films. His considerable TV work includes The Avengers, Fawlty Towers, Dr Who, Last of the Summer Wine, and Coronation Street. His voice is also familiar on TV as narrator on The Wombles, as Tufty in the road safety films, and as Busby in the Post Office telephone adverts. During the 1960s he worked with the famous Beatles Producer, George Martin, to release several comedy records including Right Said Fred and Hole In The Ground. He was appointed Officer of the Order of the British Empire (OBE) in 2011.

ABOVE – A proud Mr. Albert Perks with wife Nell and family – Photo: Canal + Image UK Ltd.

His character of Mr. Perks was a proud and stubborn Yorkshireman who would not stand for any of that "charity nonsense" despite having a wife and family to support on his meagre pay. He took great pride in his job and happily befriended the 'upper class' Waterbury family who had fallen on hard times. He helped sort out their problems and forgave occasional misdemeanours such as stealing coal from the station to keep mother warm. He offered presents of 'Sweet Briar' to the children's ill Mother and even had a small gift for Roberta's birthday. It was his well meaning gift of newspapers and magazines that led Roberta to realise the true extent of her father's plight. Perks was always there to offer friendly advice and act as a go-between in their adventures.

Love
Bernard Cribbins

On Monday 1st August 1988, Bernard Cribbins returned to the Railway to film a TV programme called 'Away Day'. This was one of a six part series in which show business personalities are asked to revisit the location of one of their past productions. Bernard chose 'The Railway Children'. The service train hauled by locomotive No. 5820 was used for many shots, with additional material filmed after the normal service. His presence at Oakworth did not go unnoticed and station staff even had to erect makeshift crowd-control barriers.

During his visit, Lancashire-born Bernard made a good-humoured entry in the Oakworth Station diary (above). The writing is a little unclear in places but he clearly enjoyed his return visit.

LEFT - Bernard Cribbins in Haworth yard during his visit in 1988 – Photo: Robin Higgins

The Railway Children at play

ABOVE - It's not all hard work. Dinah Sheridan and the 'Children' relax outside Elstree's studios in Borehamwood, now the site of a Tesco supermarket – Photo: Canal + Image UK Ltd.

BELOW – The children dance among the cables and filming paraphernalia between shots at Oakworth station – Photo: N.R. Knight

"What's that white line on the coal heap" ___

When Mother falls ill, Peter goes down to the station to get some coal to keep her warm and make her well again. When he is discovered by Mr. Perks, Peter pleads his innocence by saying, "I'm only taking it from the top, that's mining".

This photo from the film company archive shows Peter taking coal from the pile which was created opposite Oakworth goods shed. In the background is a rare glimpse of locomotive 'Lord Mayor' which featured in some of the film's publicity material and on the cover of one of the soundtrack LPs. The locomotive is now in the care of the Ingrow-based Vintage Carriages Trust.

LEFT – Peter at work 'mining' coal from Oakworth station coal yard to keep his poorly mother warm
Photo: Canal + Image UK Ltd

The coal heap at Oakworth station was actually the property of village coal merchant, Norman Feather, who had traded from the Station Goods Yard for many years and worked with wagon owner David Peel to supply the needs of locals.

When film bosses wanted a coal heap producing in Oakworth station yard, they clearly did not have far to look. David set to work to pile up coal opposite the goods shed and even painted the famous white line round the heap so that you could, as Mr. Perks put it, "See if anyone nicks any".

The Oakworth coal yard closed following Mr. Feather's retirement so David Peel took over the nearby coal merchant business in Haworth yard which he ran successfully for many years.

The business was recently taken over by David's son Andrew and still retains its original name of Hartley & Whittaker and a postal address which the phone book continues to describe as 'LMS Goods Yard'. David still pops down occasionally and is pictured here while lending a hand during the autumn of 2012 - Photo: Jim Shipley

"Oakworth, Oakworth Station"

KWVR volunteer ERIC RING recalls the struggle to prepare Oakworth Station for its starring role

Oakworth station probably survived due to the continuing presence in the goods yard of Mr. Feather the coal merchant and that of a rather colourful local who, I understand, insisted on speaking in rubbish French from his reputed world war one service. He was probably a good security guard as the place suffered little damage following closure. In due course the railway's Civil department adopted the yard and goods shed, and attention soon turned to the rather forlorn but still intact station building.

Possibly the first bit of station restoration was undertaken by some volunteers from the Ffestiniog Railway, who I seem to recall painted everything green and white. The first serious attempts began in 1969 under the guidance of Guy Henderson and his dogs, plus Gordon Massey, Graham Bentley, myself, and others lost in the mists of time. Everything was to be genuine Midland brown and cream, the ladies room and gents were to be tastefully restored, and the platform gas lamp posts reinstated.

The station building was a bit of a mess with damp everywhere, a collapsed ceiling and a rotten floor in the booking office. Guy had to fight off suggestions that it would all cost too much and should be bulldozed like Ingrow, however we plodded on with help on the big jobs from local contractor Ernest Rhodes, whose family still have a shop near Haworth station.

ABOVE – Oakworth station dressed for the BBC's 1968 TV serialisation of The Railway Children. Note the absence of gas lamp pillars at this stage – Photo: Eric Ring

It was decided that the gas lamps should be restored to their original Edwardian splendour. The sites of the old posts were easily located as BR had just sledge-hammered them at ground level. New posts were acquired from various points around the railway and after much digging a pipe was restored along the front of the platform with trenches to the lamps. Fittings such as wall brackets, lanterns (ex-Keighley Corporation) and time clocks were found and the whole thing was finally connected to the meter box.

I seem to recall that it was all a bit 'last minute' in 1970, with Eddie Stock repainting the fence in brown and laying tarmac on the new gas pipe trenches. By the time the film people arrived, everything was lovely and clean in brown and cream – so they decided to smear weathering gunk over everything. We weren't best pleased.

And now my starring role; ringing the bells. I was at Oakworth one day during the filming and Peter Handford's crew wanted to record some sound effects, including the block bell which advised staff that a train was coming. I rang the thing about a dozen times for the industrial strength reel to reel tape and that was it. My efforts were then used quite a few times in the film, the most obvious one being to wake Mr Perks at the first shot of him asleep in his chair.

The Ladies Room was used as Mr Perks' office and various props were found to add authenticity. The filing rack came from what is now Haworth loco shed mess room, while the table was previously used by Keighley booking clerks on summer Sundays during 1968 when passengers could only enter from what is now the car park. Other props included the 'Kings Cross' sign seen briefly in the film which was actually just a board with 'OSS' on it. It survived in Oakworth yard for a while after the filming, as did the famous fibreglass tree from the landslide which many believed had taken root. The props people were also kept busy down at Mytholmes where massive tarpaulins were erected at either end of the tunnel to make it seem longer, and hundreds of wooden covers were used to disguise the concrete sleepers on Mytholmes curve.

I seem to recall taking two weeks off work for the film and did night security in the Pullman and Chatham coaches in Haworth yard used as wardrobes, dressing rooms and make-up. The daytime security guard became quite adept at waking us before the studio people arrived.

After the film was released, I recall that volunteer Simon Talbot made some photo display boards which were dragged around various cinemas to publicise the railway. You couldn't send any publicity out at the time as there was a 6-week postal strike, and I assisted Simon in the South Manchester area until my Mini Van expired. I also remember appropriating some of the plastic bunting from the front of the pannier tank for the front bumper of my van.

ABOVE - The ex-GWR Pannier Tank with the bunting which eventually found its way onto Eric Ring's mini van – Photo: Eric Ring

"Peter, who wants to be an engineer" _____

JIM SHIPLEY considers the career of former child actor Gary Warren and tries to sort fact from fiction with a little help from the man himself and those who know him.

Gary Warren was born on 5th July 1954 and grew up in Neasden, London. Biographical material released by EMI in 1970 and subsequent interviews with 'TV Times' and its junior version 'Look In' reveal that Gary secured his first TV role at the age of 12 playing Pinocchio in 'Disney Wonderland'. Further work followed so he left Grammar School to attend the famous Aida Foster Stage School in Golders Green where he was able to continue his general education while studying dance and drama. A keen Queens Park Rangers fan, most of his money was spent attending football matches or buying pop records. Gary's career continued to flourish with appearances in The Charlie Drake Show, Z Cars, The Ragged Trousered Philanthropist, ITV Playhouse, Whack-O, Don't Raise The Bridge, Lower The River, I'll Never Forget What's 'Is Name and Catweazle. In 1969 he played young 'Patrick' alongside Ginger Rogers in 'Mame' at the Royal Theatre in Drury Lane. He retired from acting in the 1970s.

LEFT – Gary during filming in 1970 – Photo: Robin Higgins

Apart from 'The Railway Children', one of Gary's most famous roles was that of Cedric in TV's 'Catweazle'. Catweazle club member, Sue Duce, met Gary at the club's 2011 annual convention and told me: "Gary effectively gave up acting in the 1970s. Contrary to some internet reports, he never appeared in 'Escape from Alcatraz' - that was his American namesake Gary F. Warren. I believe his last acting job was a late 1970s BBC drama series called 'Sea Tales'. He did try his luck in America but it just didn't happen for him. I don't think he ever lived there but simply went in search of work. I think the rumours of Gary's involvement in the Canadian fur trade stem from the fact that his father was actually a furrier in London. I am pretty sure that Gary has, for the most part, lived and worked in England. I believe he was involved in a family clothing business at one stage. When I've spoken to Gary in the past, he has always said that the film was in his past and that's where it is staying. However he is a big fan of Twitter and seems to enjoy discussing 'The Railway Children' whenever it is on TV. Gary was interviewed in 2009 and 2010 by friend and BBC London 94.9 D.J. Danny Baker where he chatted informally about his roles in 'The Railway Children' and 'Catweazle' and answered listeners' questions"

RIGHT – Gary at the Catweazle Club's Annual Convention in 2011 – Photo: Sue Duce

ABOVE – Gary Warren with fellow Catweazle actor Geoffrey Bayldon - Photo: Sue Duce
BELOW – Gary and Sue Duce at the 2011 Catweazle Club Convention - Photo: Sue Duce

A **little known fact is that** Gary made a pop record shortly after his appearance in 'The Railway Children'. Released on the President label in 1971, the 'a' side is called 'Lucky Guy' and the 'b' side is called 'Jennifer Please'. He even had his own Fan Club.

Gary's nascent pop career was highlighted in the TV Times of 27th February 1971. Perhaps a little tongue in cheek, he told them, "I can't read music but I'm learning the piano and have had some singing lessons. I made my first record six years ago when I was 10. It was 'I Saw Mummy Kissing Santa Claus' and I wasn't very pleased with it. I hope this one is a lot better".

Catweazle Club member, Sue Duce, managed to acquire two copies of the record and reckons that Gary sounds a bit like Peter Noone of Herman's Hermits. She recalls, "I put one copy of the record in the club's silent auction and I've kept the other copy which Gary has kindly autographed for me".   ABOVE – Photo: Sue Duce

When Gary became aware that I was updating this book, he very kindly offered the following memories of his career and gave an insight into his current life.

ABOVE – The original 'Mame' theatre programme from 1969 – Author's Collection

"Yes I was in 'Mame' with Ginger Rogers ...... who I *DANCED* with ..... me & Fred huh! I sang the song 'My Best Girl' in the show. I learned it for the audition which may well have given me some advantage as most of the other boys sang "Consider Yourself" or some such. I did the complete 13 month run but unfortunately they didn't make an album ...... still don't know why. Ginger had a month off during the run and Juliet Prowse filled in ...... whew".

"Prior to that I was in the West End revival of Dodie Smith's 'Dear Octopus' in 1968, my only other "theatre". It had an amazing cast including Richard Todd, Cicely Courtneidge and hubby Jack Hulbert. One evening Noel Coward saw the show and came backstage. He chatted to me for a while, was most complimentary and I was totally starstruck".

"As far as memories of 'The Railway Children' filming go, the one thing that sticks in my mind is the fabulous weather up in Yorkshire when we filmed. It gave everything a magical quality and we all felt we were blessed with making a very memorable film. I have fond memories of us three kids and Dinah (Sheridan). We got on so well together that by the end we did indeed feel like a real family. Sally (Thomsett) freaked the locals out by wearing very trendy mini skirts in the evening after walking around all day in costume. I, on the other hand, turned no heads whatever I wore".

"I gave up acting a few years after the film. I'm now married nearly thirty years with two kids in their twenties – a boy (a composer and producer in the music industry) and a girl (a journalist). They're both doing great and I'm a proud dad".

"That Canada Furrier thing was always incorrect. My Dad was a furrier in the UK, but I don't know how the Canada part ever came into it".

Gary is a huge football fanatic and a lifelong fan of Queens Park Rangers. During filming for Catweazle in 1971, he and the camera crew often enjoyed a game of football between takes, though sadly he could never persuade Geoffrey Bayldon to join in.

ABOVE - Not quite Rodney Marsh, but Gary seems to be enjoying himself here back in the early 70s. Our thanks for permission to use this photo from his personal collection.

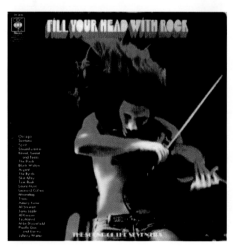

Another of Gary's great loves is music, particularly 1970s progressive rock. He told me, "It was a very important part of my growing up and music has always been a major part of my life, both listening and playing. My singing is OK but my guitar playing could still use some perfecting".

He also recalled an incident back in 1970 during filming of The Railway Children when he slipped away to a local record shop to purchase a copy of 'Fill Your Head With Rock', a double album sampler on the CBS label which he later said changed his life. The album featured Leonard Cohen, The Byrds, Janis Joplin, Taj Mahal, Argent, and many others.

Lionel Jeffries

Lionel Jeffries passed away on 19th February 2010 following a long illness. He was 83. Born in London's East End in 1926, he will be fondly remembered for his work on 'The Railway Children', but his career also included TV and stage work plus appearances in over 100 films including Two Way Stretch, The Wrong Arm of the Law, The Colditz Story, Doctor at Large, Blue Murder at St Trinians and Chitty Chitty Bang Bang – where he played Grandpa Potts.

ABOVE – Lionel Jeffries with Musical Director Johnny Douglas - Photo: Canal + Image UK Ltd

BELOW – Lionel and team while filming in Haworth village - Photo: Canal + Image UK Ltd.

There have been many richly deserved tributes to Lionel Jeffries from the world of stage and screen, but volunteers on the K&WVR will always remember that it was his work with our Railway over forty years ago that made our success possible. It made people realise that we were not just a group of eccentric amateurs doomed to inevitable failure, but that we had shown, at a time when local railways were being closed everywhere, that communities could take them over and run them successfully.

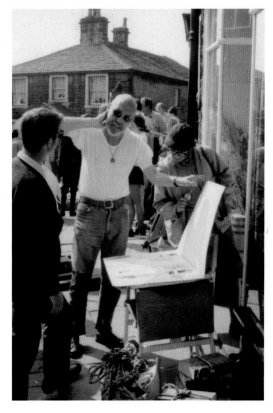

We celebrated the film's 40th anniversary during 2010 and took time to remember Lionel Jeffries and all that he, along with a superb cast and crew, did for the future of this Railway. Thanks to him, people from all over the world still come to ride on our trains and visit Oakworth station.

With the passing of Lionel Charles Jeffries, the world has lost a great actor and director, a true character, and a very fine gentleman.

Exploitation

The release of The Railway Children film in 1970 inspired several companies to issue merchandise linking their products to the film. Here a just a few examples from the early 1970s, most of which are now collectors' items.

In 1972, Triang-Hornby produced an 00 gauge train set (RS615) based on the train from the film. It included a 'Jinty' steam locomotive with 'synchrosmoke' and painted in the fictitious Great Northern & Southern Railway livery. The set also included two period coaches, an oval of track, and a station.

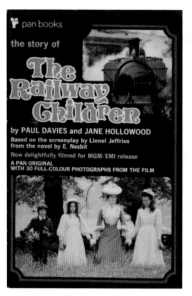

(Left) Pan Books issued a 'story of the film' paperback based on the Lionel Jeffries screenplay. It contained many colour images from the film and cost 25p.

(Right) Puffin published a new paperback edition of the original Nesbit book. It also sold for 25p and included full film credits.

Released in 1971 on the budget Music for Pleasure label as MFP 1430, this record featured a Lionel Jeffries narration of the story with excerpts of the dialogue and music

In 1970 Columbia Records produced a soundtrack Long Playing record No. SCX 6446. It featured music from the film plus a full colour picture on the sleeve with further stills and full film credits on the reverse.

Popular singing star Vince Hill recorded 'More Than Ever Now', one of the musical items from the film. It was released in 1970 as the B-side of a 45rpm 7" single on the Columbia label No. DB 8738.

Pan produced a Papersculpture Book containing text from the film and pictures together with two model engines that children could build for themselves. It cost just 75p

CALL SHEET

NO: 42

PRODUCTION: "THE RAILWAY CHILDREN"	DATE: FRIDAY, 29th MAY, 1970
LOC: TUNNEL BETWEEN OAKWORTH AND HAWORTH. (LOADING: See note at end)	UNIT CALL: 8.30 a.m. at location
SETS: 1. EXT. FENCE AND TUNNEL 2. INT. OLD GENT'S CARRIAGE	SCENE NOS: 100.101.102.112.114.116.121.122. DAY 103.113.115.118. DAY

DIRECTOR: LIONEL JEFFRIES

ARTIST	CHARACTER		D/R	M/U	ON SET
1. EXT. FENCE AND TUNNEL. Sc.Nos. 100.101.102.112.114.116.121.122. DAY					
WILLIAM MERVYN	OLD GENT			7.45	8.45
JENNY AGUTTER	BOBBIE			7.45	8.45
SALLY THOMSETT	PHYLLIS			7.45	8.45
GARY WARREN	PETER			7.45	8.45
STAND-INS:					
A.N. Other	for Mr. Mervyn	)	Pick up 7.15 a.m. Merrion		
Sandy Smith	for Miss Agutter	)	Hotel then to Railyard,		
Linda Massey	for Miss Thomsett	)	Haworth. On set		8.30
Joe Davies	for Master Warren	)			
CROWD:					
1 Man	Waiter on Old Gent's train	)	Pick up 7.15 a.m. Merrion		
3 Women)	Passengers on train	)	Hotel then to Railyard,		
5 Men)		)	Haworth. On set		8.45
PROPS:	As per script and breakdown to include pocket handkerchiefs for children, newspaper for Old Gent (Sc.100-102), hammer, nails, large sheet inscribed "LOOK OUT AT THE STATION" (Sc.112-116), Large sheet inscribed "SHE IS NEARLY WELL THANK YOU" (Sc.121.122).				
TRAINS:	OLD GENT'S TRAIN. Direction Keighley-Haworth, to be standing by at Haworth Station from 8.15 a.m.				
2. INT. OLD GENT'S CARRIAGE. Sc.Nos. 103. 113. 115. 118. DAY					
WILLIAM MERVYN	OLD GENT	)			
JENNY AGUTTER	BOBBIE	)			
SALLY THOMSETT	PHYLLIS	)	As above call		
GARY WARREN	PETER	)			
STAND-INS:					
As above call					
CROWD:					
1 Man	Waiter in Old Gent's carriage - from above call.				
PROPS:	As per script and breakdown to include dressing for Old Gent's carriage, newspaper for Old Gent and as above.				
TRAINS:	OLD GENT'S TRAIN. As above call.				
CATERING:	Tea on arrival, breaks and lunch to be taken at location for approximately 95 people. As per George Cook.				
ARTISTES TRANSPORT:					
UNIT CAR 1 (SCOTTS)	To collect Miss Agutter, Miss Thomsett and Master Warren from Parkway Hotel at 6.45 a.m. then to Merrion Hotel to collect Mr. Mervyn at 7.00 a.m. then to Railyard, Haworth.				
CROWD COACH:	To be at Merrion Hotel at 7.00 a.m. to collect Crowd and Standins to depart 7.10 a.m. sharp then to Railyard, Haworth.				
LOADING	ELECTRICAL GEAR TO BE LOADED ON TRAIN (DIESEL BUS AND TRUCK). ALL OTHER TRANSPORT TO GO TO COTTAGES AT BOTTOM OF THE ROAD WHICH LEADS TO THE TOP OF THE TUNNEL, THEN TO PARK AS INSTRUCTED.				

RICHARD DALTON, Assistant Director

A 'Call Sheet' giving comprehensive details of locations, timings, railway stock, cast, extras, locomotives etc. was produced for each day's filming – Author's Collection

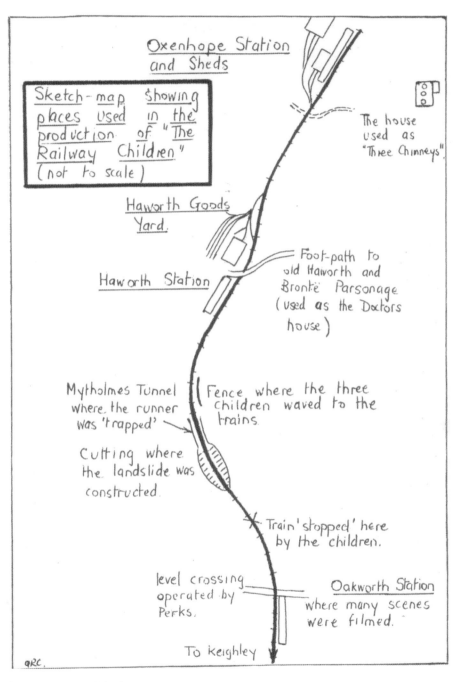

This line drawing of the filming locations was drawn by the film's 'Railway Technical Advisor', the late Bob Cryer, and first appeared in 'Worth a Second Glance – Volume 2' in the early 1970s

"Buns for tea, Mother's sold a story" _____

Dinah Sheridan was born Dinah Nadyejda Mec (pronounced 'Mess') in 1920s London to a Russian father and German mother. She trained at the famous Italia Conti School and landed her first starring role in films at the age of 15, having by now adopted the stage name of Sheridan. Following a break to concentrate on war work, she went on to make several successful films, including Get Cracking with George Formby and Genevieve with Kenneth Moore. Following a career break, she accepted the role of Mother in The Railway Children and has since appeared in numerous stage, film and TV roles including Dr. Who, Keeping Up Appearances and The Mirror Crack'd. She has been married four times: to actor Jimmy Hanley, to Sir John Davis, to John Merivale and to Aubrey Ison. Her son Jeremy Hanley became a successful accountant and politician while daughter Jenny Hanley is well remembered as an actress and presenter on children's TV's programme Magpie.

LEFT: Dinah Sheridan on set with daughter Jenny Hanley
Photo: Canal + Image UK Ltd

Dinah clearly enjoyed her time filming in Yorkshire and relished what was her first significant film role since Genevieve eighteen years earlier. On her website she even recalls, "The corsets I wore in The Railway Children are still in my undies drawer, a prized relic of my favourite film."

During the course of filming at Oakworth, keen photographer and KWVR volunteer Ken Roberts took a photograph of Dinah Sheridan resting between shots. Around 1987, Ken sent a copy of the photo to Dinah via Bob Cryer, who passed it on via Dinah's son and fellow M.P. Jeremy Hanley. Dinah was clearly taken with the photograph and was moved to write a personal letter to Ken thanking him. It reads ....

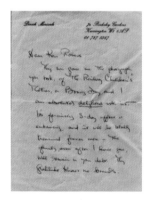

Dear Ken Roberts,

My son gave me the photograph you took of 'The Railway Children's' Mother, on Boxing Day and I am absolutely delighted with it. Its fascinating 3D effect is entrancing, and it will be totally treasured forever more. The family, even after I have gone, will remain in your debt. My gratitude knows no bounds.

How I wish we could be making the film all over again – except that I would not be chosen for the part nowadays – after 18 years. (was that really me?? – yes, I recognise the tapestry).

Thank you for giving me, and particularly my husband, such a happy start to the new year.

Warmest wishes to you.   Yours – Dinah (Sheridan)

ABOVE – This fine study of Dinah Sheridan resting between shots was taken by long standing railway volunteer Ken Roberts

Shows and Exhibitions _____

The recent 'Railway Children' centenary prompted a series of exhibitions and stage plays.

2006: The National Railway Museum in York celebrated the centenary of Nesbit's book with a half-term 'Railway Children' themed event from 22nd to 30th October 2006. Star of the show was the Old Gentleman's Saloon which was open to the public and featured the museum's own 'Old Gent' welcoming visitors on board. It was coupled to the VCT's 'Lord Mayor' – a diminutive steam locomotive which had featured in some of the film's publicity material. There were also film shows, train rides, a brass band, a paper chase, scene recreations, writers' workshops and a display of film memorabilia (much of it belonging to your author). It all made for an enjoyable addition to the museum's attractions.

2008 & 2009: Greater things were to follow when York Theatre Royal joined forces with the NRM to stage a live 'Railway Children' show at the museum. Adapted by Mike Kenny and directed by Damian Cruden, it ran for two packed summer seasons and featured a guest appearance by the NRM's Stirling Single steam locomotive.

2010: The production moved to London where it was staged in the old Eurostar terminal at Waterloo station. The Stirling Single was joined by The Old Gentleman's Saloon and many new faces joined the cast, including Marshall Lancaster as Mr. Perks. It was a huge success and the run was extended several times.

2011: The show enjoyed a successful return to Waterloo with yet more new faces, notably TV comedian Marcus Brigstocke as Mr. Perks the Porter.

ABOVE – Bernard Cribbins hands over the porter's cap to Marshall Lancaster for the 2010 run of 'The Railway Children' at Waterloo station.

Photo: Richard Davenport

RIGHT – The 1871-built North Eastern Railway Directors Saloon (The Old Gentleman's Saloon) on the M62 between Bradford and Leeds on its way to London for the 2010 stage show.

Photo: Chris Lawson

LEFT – This old bike featured in a version of the London show which was staged in Toronto during 2011. The bike returned to London in Autumn and repeated its starring role for the remainder of the London run. This truly international star may now be found at Oakworth station and is seen here with young Station Porter Sid Ashworth

Photo: Jim Shipley

RIGHT – The KWVR had a publicity and sales stand in the London Waterloo theatre concourse selling books and postcards. There was also a large photographic display.

The interval always proved a busy time. Here Chris Lawson (left) and Jim Shipley (centre) greet visitors during the 2010 run of the production.

Photo: Chris Cashman

Amateur Productions: During the last few years, many amateur dramatic groups around the country have produced stage versions of The Railway Children. A couple of local examples are shown here – Mytholmroyd St Michael's Amateurs (2009) and Silsden Community Productions (2012)

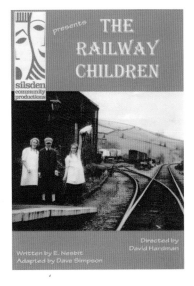

ABOVE & LEFT – The Railway has helped with the publicity material for local amateur groups staging The Railway Children

Author's Collection

"It's all uphill to Scotland

Long standing volunteer and proud Scotsman BILL BLACK recalls the summer of 1970 and how his young family rubbed shoulders with the stars.

My wife and I were comparatively new members when the filming of the Lionel Jeffries classic was made at the railway. The first job I did was to help with changing the waybeams on Bridge 16 part way round the curve that Roberta (Jenny Agutter) ran round waving her red petticoat to stop the train running into the landslide. I had trained as a Diesel Railbus driver and this enabled me to drive E79962 which was used to propel the Kirkstall Forge waggon to move camera equipment from Oakworth Station to the south side of Mytholmes tunnel for use in the scene where the harriers ran through the tunnel in the paperchase scene.

The following day I was able to take a day off work and came over to the railway with Betty and our two children Alasdair & Morag. We had brought a picnic with us and went to the field just to the south and west of Mytholmes tunnel. This was where the scenes of the children waving to the Old Gentleman (William Mervyn) were filmed as he passed in his Saloon, and where they asked him to look out at Oakworth Station so that Roberta could hand him a letter about their Father. It was a beautiful sunny day and we watched while the preparations were made for the scenes. Lionel asked for a platform to be built for the camera beside the fence at the top of the embankment and immediately a joiner (stripped to the waist) ran down the field with lengths of wood and his tool bag. In what appeared to be seconds, the platform was built.

Meanwhile the train was at Oakworth station with L89 (a GWR engine), two Metropolitan Railway coaches and the North Eastern saloon with the Old Gentleman seated at a window to the rear of the coach. We watched as these scenes were shot with the train running up towards Haworth and back towards Oakworth until the Director had all the shots he wanted. I managed to take several shots of the train movements and, during a break in filming, we had a bonus when I took a shot of our two children with Jenny Agutter.

Betty had been in Haworth Yard where two Pullman cars, Zena and one now named Mary, were used as dressing rooms for the stars. Betty had made tea for some of the actors and had a conversation with William Mervyn. He said that he did not know if what he had done with his career in acting was meaningful. This was challenged by Betty who said that he had given pleasure to millions of people who he would never know or ever meet. What more could anybody achieve in their lifetime? He was quite touched by this conversation and kissed Betty on the cheek. As Betty said, he came across on film and TV as a real gentleman and he was just the same off the set.

LEFT – Jenny Agutter with Bill's children Alasdair and Morag – Photo: Bill Black

ABOVE – This is the view that Bill and his family will have had as the train passes the camera which sits on top of the hastily assembled wooden platform – Photo: Brian Baker

BELOW – Bill's railbus ferries equipment around while the local fire brigade prepare to provide the 'torrential rain' for the arrival of the Shabby Russian – Photo: Martin Welch

Celebrating the Film's Anniversary _____

Over the years, many of the film's stars have returned to the Railway to help celebrate notable anniversaries or attend local charity functions. We have welcomed Jenny Agutter, Sally Thomsett, Bernard Cribbins and Iain Cuthbertson, and we entertain hopes that some of the other stars may be visiting us in the not too distant future.

Sally Thomsett and Jenny Agutter returned to the Railway for the film's 20th anniversary celebrations in 1990. Above at a rather busy Oakworth station and below on board the Old Gentleman's Saloon with Ann Cryer, wife of the late Bob Cryer – Photos: Ann Cryer

ABOVE – Sally Thomsett and her daughter. Charlotte, meet Keighley Mayor Margaret Ward at Oakworth Station during the 2010 'Railway Children Weekend' – Photo: David Petyt

BELOW – Jenny Agutter visited Oakworth station in 2006 as patron of the Cystic Fibrosis Trust while attending the annual Charity Funday in Haworth Park – Photo: Ian Palmer

"The End" _____

For the film's final scene, many of the actors gathered at Ebor Lane Bridge near Haworth to wave goodbye while Jenny Agutter held a blackboard upon which was written 'The End'. Thanks to a long forgotten photo in the film company archive, we can now reveal what was actually written on the other side of that blackboard.   Both photos: Canal + Image UK Ltd